To mum,

Enjoy! Happy birt[...]
& lots of lov[...]

Fraser xx

27/7/96.

Russian Lace Patterns

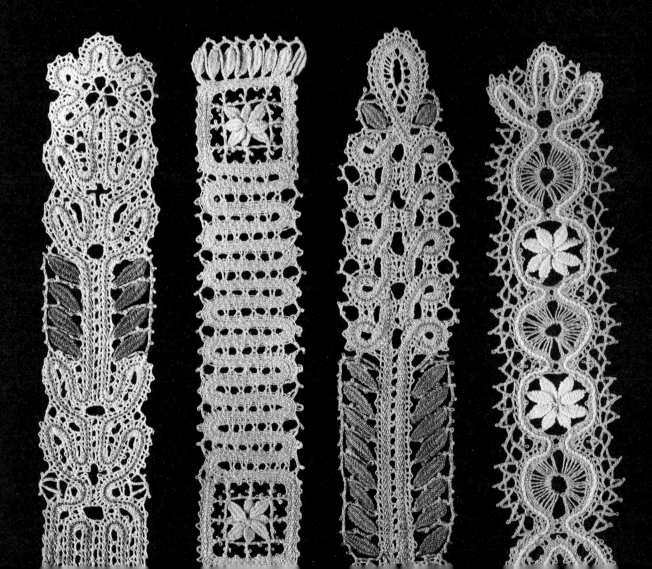

Russian Lace Patterns

Anna Korableva · Bridget M. Cook

B.T. Batsford Ltd • London

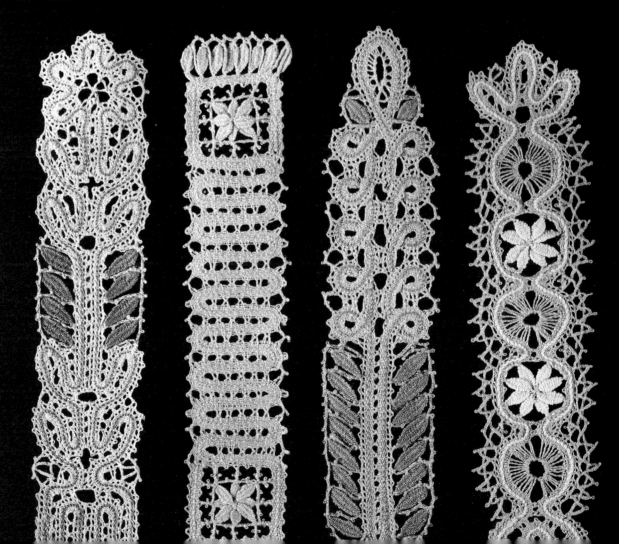

First published 1996

© Anna Korableva, Bridget M. Cook 1996

Translations by Puck Smelter-Hoekstra (Dutch)
and Margarete Wenzel (French and German)

Printed by Butler & Tanner,
Frome, Somerset

for the Publisher

B.T. Batsford Ltd
4 Fitzhardinge Street
London
W1H 0AH

A catalogue record for this book is available from
the British Library

ISBN 0 7134 6792 4

CONTENTS

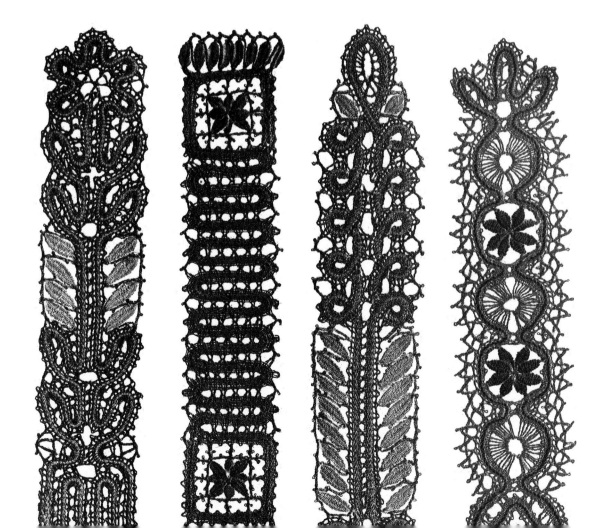

PREFACE

Russian lacemaking has a history which is centuries old, with patterns and terms that are both ancient and unique. Mention of lacemaking in Russia is found as early as the thirteenth century.

The oldest examples were made from metallic gold and silver thread for the adornment of ecclesiastical vestments, and for the robes of the Tsar and his family. To this day traditional ways of naming measured lace are retained in such names as little coin, copecks, little wheel, birch tree, little star, little pearl, crow and frost. On antique Russian lace, on items such as covers and trimmings for clothes and towels, one meets motifs of peacocks and birds perched on flowering bushes, each with fascinating and highly technical detail. From the fifteenth century onwards, lace was made from linen flax, usually in white thread. Later, additional coloured silk began to be used in Russian lace construction.

In the nineteenth century linen tape lace was woven with additional coloured threads for the decoration of peasant clothing and linens. Fairy tales, fantastic peacocks, flowers, human figures and geometrical ornaments were depicted in linen lace. In very old lace, which used the tape technique of weaving, there was no background work. The earliest lace with a background was made in the first half of the nineteenth century.

At the end of the 1920s and the beginning of the 1930s, the character of lacemaking in Russia changed dramatically. Many new subjects for composition were created. Representations of Soviet emblems and architectural motifs appeared, originally linked with the older patterns of Russian lace, in which the richness of Russian lace patterns were revealed.

Anna Korableva later created a number of unique works inspired by this period. A curtain, 'Tiled pattern', a panel, 'Sputnik', a table-cloth, 'White squirrel', and the panels 'Matrioshka' and 'The uniting of the Ukraine with Russia'; in the latter the beauty of Russian architecture is conveyed in images. The panel 'Russian motifs' won the Grand-Prix award in the 1958 Brussels international exhibition.

Until 1935, Russian lace was manufactured mainly for export. In the second half of the 1930s the development of lacemaking was rapid, especially with the creation of new ornaments and technical methods.

The artists of the Scientific Research Institute of Art and Industry and of Vologda, Yelts and Kirov were responsible for the creation of new folk ornaments. Artists and lace craftpersons were particularly successful in the post-war years, when their full attention was directed to the creation of lace piece-making. At that time a number of unique works were created at the Scientific Research Institute, and ornaments of elaborate Russian tape lace can be discovered in these pieces.

Today, the art of lace-making has become one of the most significant types of Soviet decorative art.

VOORWOOD

Kant in Rusland heeft een eeuwenoude geschiedenis, met patronen en uitdrukkingen die zowel klassiek als uniek zijn. Al in de dertiende eeuw is sprake van het maken van kant in Rusland.

De oudste voorbeelden waren gemaakt van goud- en zilverdraad, voor de versiering van kerkelijke gewaden en voor de kleding van de Tsaar en zijn familie. Tot op de dag van vandaag zijn traditionele benamingen van meterkant behouden in namen als: kleine munt, kopeken, klein wiel, beukeboom, kleine ster, kleine parel, kraai en vorst. Op antieke Russische kant vindt men, op stukken als hoezen/lakens en garnering voor kleding en handdoeken, motieven met pauwen en vogels op bloeiende struiken, allemaal met fascinerende en technische zeer fraaie details. Na de vijftiende eeuw werd kant gemaakt van, meestal wit, linnen. Later begon men gekleurde zijde toe te voegen bij het maken van Russische kant.

In de negentiende eeuw werd linnen bandkant gemaakt voor de versiering van boerenkleding en linnengoed, waarbij gekleurde draden werden toegevoegd. Sprookjes, fantastische pauwen, bloemen, mensfiguren en geometrische ornamenten werden afgebeeld in linnen kant. Zeer oude kant, waarin de slingerende bandjes werden gebruikt, had geen achtergrond. De vroegste kant met een achtergrond werd gemaakt in de eerste helft van de negentiende eeuw.

Aan het eind van de twintiger en het begin van de dertiger jaren veranderde het karakter van de kant in Rusland dramatisch. Er onstonden veel nieuwe onderwerpen voor kunstwerken. Voorstellingen van Sovjetemblemen en architectonische motieven verschenen, oorspronkelijk verbonden met de oude patronen voor Russische kant, waarin de rijkdom van de Russische patronen getoond werd.

Anna Korableva heeft later een aantal unieke stukken gemaakt die door die periode zejn geinspireerd. Een gordijn, "Tegelpatroon", een wandkleed, "Spoetnik", een tafelkleed, "Witte eekhoorn", en de wandkleden "Matrioshka" en "De vereniging van de Oekraïne met Rusland"; in het laatste wordt de schoonheid van de Russische architectuur uitgedrukt in de afbeeldingen. Het wandkleed "Russische motieven" won de Grand-Prix in de Brusselse internationale tentoonstelling van 1958.

Tot 1935 werd kant in Rusland voornamelijk gemaakt voor de export. In de tweede helft van de dertiger jaren ontwikkelde het maken van kant zich snel, vooral door het creëren van nieuwe ornamenten en technische methoden.

De kunstenaars van het Scientific Research Institute of Art and Industry (Wetenschappelijk Onderzoeksinstituut voor Kunst en Industrie) en van Vologda, Yelts en Kirov waren verantwoordelijk voor het scheppen van nieuwe volksornamenten. Kunstenaars en kantwerk(-st)ers hadden vooral veel succes in de na-oorlogse jaren, toen hun volle aandacht was gericht op het creëren van kantwerken. In die tijd zijn een aantal unieke stukken gemaakt in het Scientific Research Institute (Wetenschappelijk Onderzoeksinsituut). In deze stukken zijn ornamenten van ingewikkelde Russische bandkant te vinden.

Tegenwoordig is de kunst van het kantmaken één van de belangrijkste Sovjet schone kunsten.

PRÉFACE

La dentelle russe peut s'enorgueiller d'une histoire vieille de plusieurs siècles, avec des dessins et des termes qui sont aussi anciens qu'uniques. On trouve des mentions de dentelle russe déjà au treizième siècle.

Les modèles les plus anciens étaient exécutés en fils métalliques or et argent pour garnir des vêtements sacerdotaux et les robes du Tsar et de sa famille. Jusqu'à nos jours se sont conservées les appellations traditionnelles de la dentelle au mètre dans les termes tels que petite monnaie, copeks, petite roue, bouleau, petite étoile, petite perle, corneille et gel. Sur la vieille dentelle russe, sur des ouvrages tels que couvertures et garnitures pour vêtements et linge de maison, on trouve des motifs de paons et d'oiseaux perchés sur des buissons fleuris, chacun avec ses détails fascinants de haute technicité. A partir du quinzième siècle, la dentelle était faite en fil de lin, habituellement en blanc. Plus tard, de la soie en couleurs était ajoutée à la composition de la dentelle russe.

Au dix-neuvième siècle, la dentelle en bandes exécutée en lin avec des fils de soie de couleurs supplémentaires, était utilisée pour agrémenter les vêtements et le linge des paysans. Des contes de fée, des paons de fantaisie, des fleurs, des représentations d'hommes et des ornements géométriques formaient le décor des dentelles en lin. Dans la dentelle très ancienne, qui utilisait déjà la technique des bandes, il n'y a aucun travail de fond. C'est la première moitié du dix-neuvième siècle qui a vu naître la première dentelle avec un fond.

Autour de 1930 on observe un changement radical dans la fabrication des dentelles. Une grande quantité de nouveaux sujets de composition apparaissent et on trouve des représentations d'emblèmes soviétiques et des motifs architecturaux, à l'origine liés aux dessins plus anciens du patrimoine russe qui révélaient la richesse artistique des dentelles russes.

Anna Korableva a créé plus tard un certain nombre d'ouvrages uniques inspirés par cette période: un rideau, "Dessin de tuiles", un panneau, "Sputnik", une nappe, "Ecureuil blanc", et les panneaux "Matrioschka" et "Unification de l'Ukraine avec la Russie"; dans ce dernier est exprimée la beauté de l'architecture russe. Un panneau "Motifs russes" a été récompensé par le Grand Prix à l'Exposition Internationale à Bruxelles en 1958.

Jusqu'en 1935, la dentelle russe avait été fabriquée principalement pour l'exportation. Dans la seconde moitié des années trente, elle a subi un développement rapide avec la création de nouveaux motifs d'ornements et de méthodes techniques.

Les artistes de l'Institut de Recherches Scientifiques pour l'Art et l'Industrie des villes de Vologda, Yelts et Kirov étaient chargés de la création de nouveaux motifs folkloriques. Ensemble avec les dentellières ils fournissaient un travail particulièrement réussi dans les années d'après-guerre, quand toute leur attention était concentrée sur la création de la dentelle. A cette époque, un certain nombre de travaux uniques a été créé à l'Institut des Recherches Scientifiques et on y découvre des motifs élaborés de la dentelle russe en bandes.

De nos jours, l'art de faire de la dentelle est devenu une des branches les plus significatives de l'art décoratif soviétique.

VORWORT

Die russische Spitze kann auf eine Jahrhunderte alte Tradition zurückblicken und bietet Muster und Arbeitsweisen, die nicht nur alt, sondern auch einmalig sind. Bereits im 13. Jahrhundert wird die russische Spitze in Schriften erwähnt.

Die ältesten Beispiele waren mit goldenen und silbernen Metallfäden zur Verzierung von Priestergewändern und der Bekleidung des Zaren und seiner Familie geklöppelt. Bis zum heutigen Tage erhielten sich die traditionellen Bezeichnungen von Meterspitze in Namen wie kleine Münze, Kopeken, kleines Rad, Birkenbaum, kleiner Stern, kleine Perle, Krähe und Frost. Auf alten russischen Spitzen, wie Decken, Kleidungs- und Handtuchsverzierungen, findet man Pfauenmuster und Vögel auf blühenden Büschen, alle mit faszinierenden und technisch sehr verfeinerten Einzelheiten. Seit dem 15. Jahrhundert wurden die Spitzen mit Leinenflachs geklöppelt, und zwar meistenteils in Weiss. Später begann man, zusätzliche bunte Seide im Aufbau der russischen Spitze zu verwenden.

Im 19. Jahrhundert wurden Leindenbandspitzen zum Schmuck von Bauernbekleidung und -wäsche auch mit farbigen Fäden angefertigt. Märchenmotive, phantasiereiche Pfauen, Blumen, menschliche Gestalten und geometrische Figuren erschienen auf der Leinenspitze. Sehr alte Spitzen, die die Klöppelart der Bandspitze benutzen, weisen keinen Hintergrund auf. Die früheste Spitze mit Grundmotiven stammt aus der ersten Hälfte des 19. Jahrhunderts.

Am Ende der zwanziger Jahre und zu Beginn der dreissiger Jahre unseres Jahrhunderts änderte sich die Spitzenklöppelei drastisch. Viele neue Musterelemente kamen auf. Sowjetabzeichen und Baudenkmäler erschienen auf den Spitzen, ursprünglich im Zusammenhang mit älteren Mustern, in denen der Reichtum russischer Spitzenkunst offenbar wurde.

Nach dem Einfluß jener Zeit schuf Anna Korableva eine Anzahl einmaliger Werke: einen Vorhang, "Dachziegelmuster", einen Wandbehang, "Sputnik", eine Tischdecke, "Weisses Eichhörnchen", und die Wandbehänge "Matrioschka" und "Vereinigung der Ukraine mit Russland"; in dem zuletzt genannten Werk kommt die Schönheit russischer Architektur zur Geltung. Der Wandbehang "Russische Motive" gewann den ersten Preis bei der Weltausstellung von Brüssel im Jahre 1958.

Bis zum Jahre 1935 wurde die russische Spitze hauptsächlich für den Export geklöppelt. In der zweiten Hälfte der dreissiger Jahre entwickelte sich die Spitzenklöppelei rapide, besonders durch die Schaffung neuer Ornamente und technischer Methoden.

Die Künstler des wissenschaftlichen Forschungsinstitutes für Kunst und Industrie in Vologda, Yelts und Kirov waren für die Schaffung neuer volkstümlicher Ornamente verantwortlich. Künstler und Klöpplerinnen erzielten besondere Erfolge in den Nachkriegsjahren, als ihr ganzes Augenmerk auf die Schaffung neuer Klöppelkreationen gerichtet war. Zu dieser Zeit entstand eine Anzahl einmaliger Werke am wissenschaftlichen Forschungsinstitut, und man kann in ihnen Ornamente von hoch entwickelten Bandspitzen finden.

Heute ist die Kunst des Klöppelns von Spitzen eine der bedeutendsten Zweige sowjetischer dekorativer Kunst.

TECHNICAL ASSISTANCE

TAPE A

A twisted gimp pair on the outer edge of the central passive pairs, plus twisted edge pairs on either side of the tape.

TAPE B

A twisted gimp pair in the centre of the passive pairs, plus twisted edge pairs on either side of the tape.

TAPE C

Clothstitched gimp pair on the outer edge of the central passives, plus twisted edge pairs on either side of the tape.

TAPE D

Clothstitched gimp pair in the centre of the passive pairs plus twisted edge pairs on either side of the tape.

TAPE E

Chevron gimp pairs on the outer edge of the central passive pairs, plus twisted edge pairs on either side of the tape.

TAPE F

Chevron gimp pairs in the centre of the passive pairs, plus twisted edge pairs on either side of the tape.

TAPE G

The gimp pair is clothstitched down the centre of the passive pairs. There are no twisted edge pairs: only the worker pair is twisted around the pins.

TAPE H

The gimp pair is clothstitched down the centre of the tape, plus twisted edge pairs on either side of the tape.

Filling notes for backgrounds

Filling note no. 1

One thread of the gimp pair can be woven to the edge, and with one thread from the edge pair becomes a mixed pair. With this mixed pair and the weaver pair, make the filling using the gimp thread as the weaver for the leaves. This gimp thread is then returned to its original position before the tape continues.

Filling note no. 2

The filling of plaits, picots and leaves is made in zig zag lines, and joined wherever the zig zags meet either themselves or the lace with sewings. (Fig. 1)

Filling note no. 3

The filling of plaits, picots and leaves are worked in straight lines, turning along the edges, back and forth. When the two plaits cross each other or meet the lace, a sewing is made to connect them. (Fig. 2)

Filling note no. 4

The plaits and picots are worked in triangles and are joined to the lace with sewings.

The patterns

All patterns have been reduced to half size. They therefore need to be enlarged to 200% before use.

The threads

Threads used were between 35/2 and 100/2.

Gimp threads can be cotton perlé, viscose, silk or metallic thread as required by the lacemaker for each individual pattern.

The majority of the patterns in this book were made in linen thread, unless otherwise stated. However, the thickness of linen thread varies with different manufacturers. To select the correct thickness of thread it is suggested that the lacemaker experiment by first making a small section of the pattern in the thread of their choice, and then deciding whether this is satisfactory enough to be used for the complete pattern.

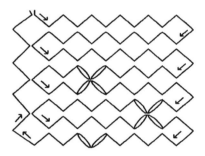

Fig. 1

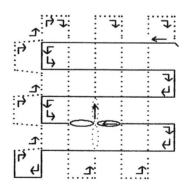

Fig. 2

TECHNISCHE HULP

BANDJE A
Een gedraaid sierdraadpaar aan de buitenkant van de middelste hangende paren, plus gedraaide randparen aan beide zijden van het bandje.

BANDJE B
Een gedraaid sierdraadpaar in het midden tussen de hangende paren, plus gedraaide randparen aan beide zijden van het bandje.

BANDJE C
Sierdraadpaar in linnenslag aan de buitenkant van de middelste hangende paren, plus gedraaide randparen aan beide zijden van het bandje.

BANDJE D
Sierdraadpaar in linnenslag midden tussen de hangende paren plus gedraaide randparen aan beide zijden van het bandje.

BANDJE E
Sierdraadparen in kettingsteek aan de buitenkant van de middelste hangende paren, plus gedraaide randparen aan beide zijden van het bandje.

BANDJE F
Sierdraadparen in kettingsteek midden tussen de hangende paren, plus gedraaide randparen aan beide zijden van het bandje.

BANDJE G
Het sierdraadpaar gaat in linnenslag door het midden van de hangende paren. Er zijn geen gedraaide randparen: alleen het looppaar wordt om de spelden gedraaid.

BANDJE H
Het sierdraadpaar gaat in linnenslag door het midden van het bandje, plus gedraaide randparen aan beide zijden van het bandje.

Aanwijzingen voor de vulling van de achtergronden.

Vullingaanwijzing nr. 1
Eén draad van het sierdraadpaar kan in linnenslag naar de rand gebracht worden, en vormt daar met één draad van het randpaar een gemengd paar. Maak met dit gemengde paar en het looppaar de vulling en gebruik daarbij de sierdraad als loper in de blaadjes. Daarna gaat deze sierdraad weer naar zijn oude plaats, voordat het bandhje verder gaat.

Vullingaanwijzing nr. 2
De vulling van vlechten, picots en blaadjes wordt gemaakt in zigzaglijnen, en aangehaakt telkens waar de zigzaglijnen elkaar of de kant ontmoeten. (Fig. 1)

Vullingaanwijzing nr. 3
De vulling van vlechten, picots an blaadjes wordt gewerkt in rechte lijnen, die langs de randen keren. Waar de twee vlechten elkaar kruisen of de kant raken, worden ze door een aanhaking verbonden. (Fig. 2)

Vullingsaanwijzing nr. 4
De vlechten en picots worden in driehoeken gewerkt en aan de kant aangehaakt.

De patronen
Alle patronen in dit boek zijn verkleind tot de halve grootte.

Ze moeten dus an 200% vergroot worden voor het gebruik.

De gebruikte
De gebruikte garens variëren van 35/2 tot 100/2.

Sierdraden kunnen cotten perlé, viscose, zijde of metaaldraad zijn. De kantwerk(st)er kan ze voor elk patroon naar eigen smaak kiezen.

De meeste patronen in dit boek zijn, tenzij anders is aangegeven, in linnen garen geklost. Gelijke dikteaanduiding voor de linnen garens geeft echter bij de verschillende fabrikanten niet precies dezelfde dikte. Om de juiste garendikte te vinden, adviseren wij de kantwerk(-st)er een klein proefstukje te maken en zo de juiste draad te kiezen voor het uitgezochte patroon.

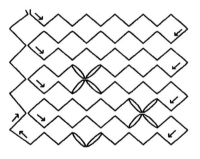

Fig. 1

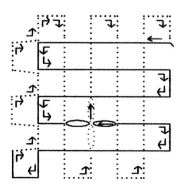

Fig. 2

ASSISTANCE TECHNIQUE

BANDE A

Tordre la paire des cordons au bord extérieur des paires passives centrales ainsi que les paires au bord de chaque côté de la bande.

BANDE B

Tordre la paire des cordons au centre des paires passives ainsi que les paires au bord de chaque côté de la bande.

BANDE C

Travailler en mat la paire des cordons au bord extérieur des paires passives centrales et tordre les paires au bord de chaque côté de la bande.

BANDE D

Travailler en mat la paire des cordons au milieu des paires passives et tordre les paires au bord de chaque côté de la bande.

BANDE E

La paire des cordons au bord extérieur des paires passives centrales est travaillée en chevrons et les paires au bord de chaque côté de la bande sont tordues.

BANDE F

Travailler les paires de cordons au centre des paires passives en chevrons et tordre les paires au bord de chaque côté de la bande.

BANDE G

La paire des cordons traverse le centre des paires passives en mat tout le long de la bande. Ne pas tordre les paires de la bordure: seulement les meneurs sont tordus autour des épingles.

BANDE H

La paire des cordons est travaillée en mat au centre de la bande et les paires au bord sont tordues de chaque côté de la bande.

Remplissage des fonds.

Remplissage no. 1

Un fil de la paire des cordons peut être ramené vers le bord pour former une paire mélangée avec un fil de la paire du bord. C'est cette paire mélangée et les meneurs qui font le remplissage en utilisant le fil des cordons comme meneur pour les feuilles. Ramener ce fil des cordons à sa position d'origine avant de continuer la bande.

Remplissage no. 2

Le remplissage formé de cordes de 4, pointons et feuilles est fait en lignes zig-zag que l'on crochète entre elles ou à la dentelle. (Dessin 1)

Remplissage no. 3

Le remplissage formé de cordes de 4, pointons et feuilles est réalisé en lignes droites qui contournent les bords en aller retour. Quand une corde de 4 rencontre une autre corde ou la dentelle, il convient de les raccorder par un crochetage. (Dessin 2)

Remplissage no. 4

Les cordes de 4 avec les pointons sont travaillées en triangles et reliées à la dentelle par crochetage.

Les modèles

Tous les modèles de ce livre ont été reduits à demi-taille. Alors, on faut les agrandir à 200% avant d'usage.

Les fils

Les fils utilisés se situent entre 35/2 et 100/2.

Pour les cordons, la dentellière peut prendre du coton perlé, de la viscose, de la soie ou des fils métalliques selon ses préférences par rapport à chaque modèle.

La majorité des modèles de ce livre a été exécutée en fil de lin s'il n'y a pas d'autre indication. Toutefois, la grosseur du fil varie selon les fabricants. Afin de trouver la grosseur appropriée, il est conseillé à la dentellière de faire un échantillon avec une partie de la dentelle choisie pour trouver le bon fil.

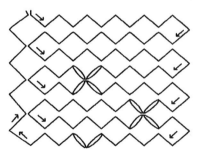

Dessin 1

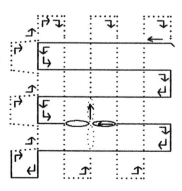

Dessin 2

TECHNISCHE HILFE

BAND A
Ein gedrehtes Konturfadenpaar am äusseren Rand der mittleren Risspaare und gedrehte Randpaare an beiden Seiten des Bandes.

BAND B
Ein gedrehtes Konturfadenpaar in der Mitte des Risspaare und gedrehte Randpaare an jeder Bandseite.

BAND C
Konturfadenpaar im Leinenschlag am äusseren Rand der mittleren Risspaare und gedrehte Randpaare an beiden Bandseiten.

BAND D
Konturfadenpaar im Leinenschlag in der Mitte der Risspaare und gedrehte Randpaare an beiden Bandseiten.

BAND E
Konturfadenpaare im Fischgräten-muster am äusseren Rand der mittleren Risspaare und gedrehte Randpaare an beiden Seiten des Bandes.

BAND F
Konturfadenpaare im Fischgräten-muster in der Mitte der Risspaare und gedrehte Randpaare an beiden Bandseiten.

BAND G
Das Konturfadenpaar durchläuft im Leinenschlag die Mitte der Risspaare. Keine gedrehten Randpaare, nur das Laufpaar wird um die Nadel gedreht.

BAND H
Das Konturfadenpaar läuft im Leinenschlag in der Mitte und gedrehte Randpaare an beiden Seiten des Bandes.

Anmerkungen zum Ausfüllen von Gründen

Grund Nr. 1
Ein Faden des Konturfadenpaares kann bis zum Rand geklöppelt werden und mit einem Faden des Randpaares ein Mischpaar bilden. Mit Läuferpaar und Mischpaar klöppelt man den Grund, wobei der Konturfaden als Läufer für die Blätter benutzt wird. Der Konturfaden wird dann in seine ursprüngliche Stellung zurückgebracht, bevor man das Band weiterklöppelt.

Grund Nr. 2
Der Grund aus Flechtern, Picots und Blättern wird in Zick-Zak-Linien ausgeführt und dort angehäkelt, wo die Zick-Zack-Linien aneinander oder an die Spitze stossen. (Abbildung 1)

Grund Nr. 3
Der Grund aus Flechtern, Picots und Blättern wird in geraden Linien geklöppelt und läuft hin und her an den Rändern entlang. Wo die Flechter sich treffen oder an die Spitze stossen, werden sie angehäkelt. (Abbildung 2)

Grund Nr. 4
Die Flechter mit Picots werden in Dreiecken ausgeführt und an die Spitze gehäkelt.

Das muster
Alle Muster in diesem Buch wurden auf die halbe Naturgrösse reduziert. Sie müssen daher vor dem Klöppeln um 200% vergrössert werden.

Die garne
Die benutzten Garne haben eine Stärke von 35/2 bis 100/2.

Als Konturfäden kann die Klöpplerin je nach Wunsch Baumwoll-Perlgarn, Viskose, Seide oder Metallfäden benutzen.

Der grösste Teil der Muster dieses Buches ist in Leinengarn geklöppelt, soweit nicht anders angegeben. Die Stärke des Leinengarns ist jedoch je nach Hersteller unterschiedlich. Um die richtige Garnstärke zu ermitteln, raten wir der Klöpplerin, zunächst einen Versuch mit einem Teil der ausgesuchten Spitze zu machen, damit sie sich für die angemessene Garnstärke entscheiden kann.

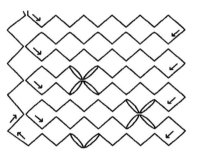

Abbildung 1

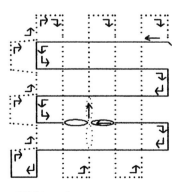

Abbildung 2

13

SONGBIRD

Bobbins: 5 pairs plus 1 extra pair for frame (cotton)
Gimps: 1 pair

Work tape B except in the half stitch section, where the gimp threads are moved over to the outside edge of the central passives and returned to the centre in the cloth-stitched areas. The extra pair is added for the frame.
Background: Filling note no. 1.

ZANGVOGEL

Klossen: 5 paar plus 1 paar (katoen)
Sierdraden: 1 paar

Werk bandje B behalve in het net-slaggedeelte, waar de sierdraden naar de buitenkant van de middelste hangende paren worden gebracht en weer naar het midden terug in de linnenslag gedeelten.
   Het extra paar is toegevoegd voor de omlijsting.

Achtergrond: vullingaanwijzing nr. 1.

OISEAU CHANTEUR

Fuseaux: 5 paires plus 1 paire (coton)
Cordons: 1 paire

Faire la bande B sauf dans la partie en grille où les cordons sont ramenés vers le bord extérieur des paires passives du centre et retournent au centre dans les parties en mat.
   Une paire supplémentaire est ajoutée pour le cadre.

Fond: Remplissage no. 1.

SINGVOGEL

Klöppel: 5 Paare plus 1 Paar (Baumwolle)
Konturfäden: 1 Paar

Band B ausführen, mit Ausnahme des Netzgrundabschnitts, wo die Konturfäden zum äusseren Rand der mittleren Risspaare hin und zurück zur Mitte des Leinenschlagabschnitts geklöppelt werden.
   Das zusätzliche Paar wird für den Rahmen verwendet.

Füllung: Grund Nr. 1.

STRUTTING PHEASANT

Bobbins: 5 pairs plus 1 extra pair for frame
Gimps: 1 pair

Work tape A; add the extra pair
for the background frame.
Background: Filling note no. 3.

PRONKENDE FAZANT

Klossen: 5 paar plus 1 paar
Sierdraden: 1 paar

Klos bandje A; voeg het extra paar toe
voor achtergrondomlijsting.

Achtergrond: vullingaanwijzing nr. 3.

FAISAN ORGUEILLEUX

Fuseaux: 5 paires plus 1 paire
Cordons: 1 paire

Faire la bande A; ajouter la paire supplémentaire pour le cadre de remplissage.

Fond: Remplissage no. 3.

STOLZER FASAN

Klöppel: 5 Paare plus 1 Paar
Konturfäden: 1 Paar

Band A klöppeln; das zusätzliche Paar für
den Rahmen des Hintergrundes benutzen.

Füllung: Grund Nr. 3.

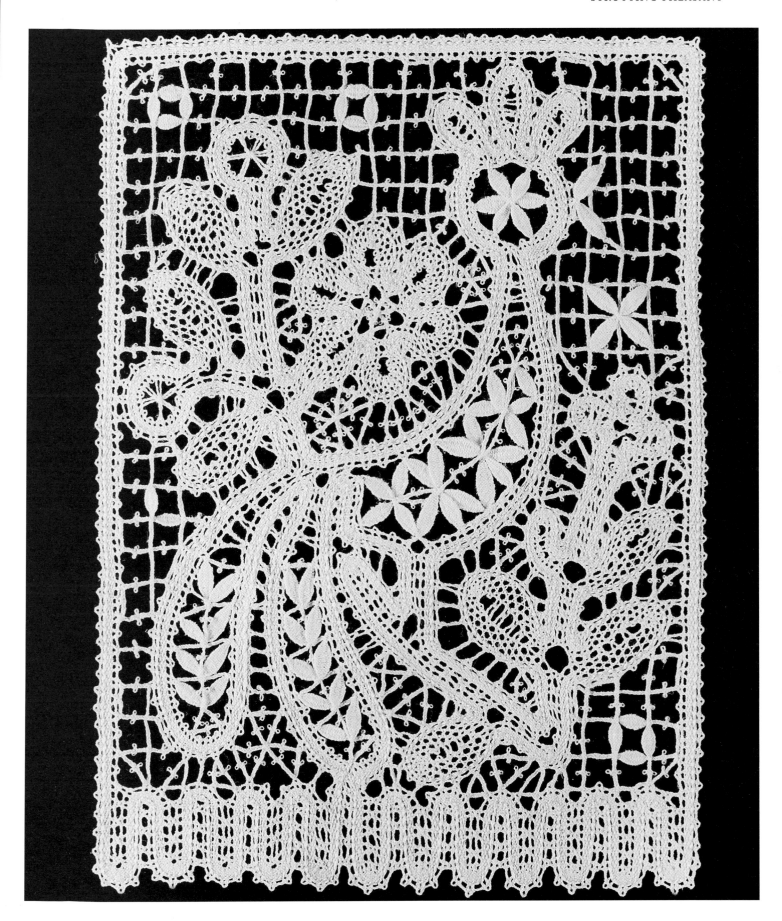

LITTLE BIRD

Bobbins: 5 pairs
Gimps: 1 pair

Work tape C. New tape C's are started for the scalloped edges.

Background: Filling note no. 2.

KLEIN VOGELTJE

Klossen: 5 paar
Sierdraden: 1 paar

Klos bandje C. Voor beide golvende randen worden nieuwe bandjes C begonnen.

Achtergrond: vullingaanwijzing nr. 2.

PETIT OISEAU

Fuseaux: 5 paires
Cordons: 1 paire

Faire la bande C. Commencer d'autres bandes C pour les deux bords à coquilles.

Fond: Remplissage no. 2.

KLEINER VOGEL

Klöppel: 5 Paare
Konturfäden: 1 Paar

Band C anwenden. Neue C-Bänder für beide Ränder in Fächer-Form beginnen.

Füllung: Grund Nr. 4.

EASTER CHICK

Bobbins: 5 pairs
Gimps: 1 pair

Work tape A.
Background: Filling note no. 4.

PAASKUIKEN	POUSSIN DE PAQUES	OSTERKUKEN
Klossen: 5 paar	Fuseaux: 5 paires	Klöppel: 5 Paare
Sierdraden: 1 paar	Cordons: 1 paire	Konturfäden: 1 Paar
Klos bandje A.	Faire la bande A.	Band A klöppeln.
Achtergrond: vullingaanwijzing nr. 4.	Fond: Remplissage no. 4.	Füllung: Grund Nr. 4.

MATRYOSHKA

Bobbins: 5 pairs
Gimps: 1 pair

Work tape B.
See filling note no. 1 for the inside of the figure.
Use Fig. 1 as a guide to working the background
filling. Work the plaits around a pin until the
opposite plaits meet.

Connect with sewings.

Fig. 1

MATRYOSHKA

Klossen: 5 paar
Sierdraden: 1 paar

Klos bandje B.

Zie vullingaanwijzing nr. 1 voor de
binnenkant van de figuur.

Gebruik Fig.1 als leidraad bij het werken
van de achtergrondvulling. Klos de vlechten
rond een speld totdat de tegenoverliggende
vlecht ook tot die speld is gewerkt.

Verbind ze door aan te haken.

MATRIOSCHKA

Fuseaux: 5 paires
Cordons: 1 paire

Faire la bande B.

Se reporter au remplissage no. 1 pour
l'intérieur du motif.

Le dessin 1 montre comment remplir le
fond. Faire les cordes du 4 autour d'une
épingle jusqu'à rencontrer la corde de
4 opposée.

Assembler par crochetage.

MATRIOSCHKA

Klöppel: 5 Paare
Konturfäden: 1 Paar

Band B klöppeln.

Siehe Grunde Nr. 1 für das Innere
der Figur. Abb. 1 zeigt, wie der Grund
auszufüllen ist. Die Flechter werden
um die Nadel gearbeitet, bis sie auf den
gegenüberliegenden Flechter stossen.

Durch Anhäkeln verbinden.

VYATSKII DOLL IN FRAME

Bobbins: 5 pairs
Gimps: 1 pair

Work tape A.
Use filling note no. 1
for the inside of the doll.

Use filling note no. 3
for the background.

VYATSKII POP IN LIJST

Klossen: 5 paar
Sierdraden: 1 paar

Klos bandje A.

Gebruik vullingaanwijzing nr. 1 voor de
binnenkant van de pop. Gebruik vullingaanwijzing nr. 2 voor de achtergrond.

POUPEE VYATSKII ENCADREE

Fuseaux: 5 paires
Cordons: 1 paire

Faire la bande A.

Utiliser le remplissage no. 1 pour l'intérieur
de la poupée et le remplissage no. 3 pour
le fond.

VYATSKII-PUPPE MIT RAHMEN

Klöppel: 5 Paare
Konturfäden: 1 Paar

Band A verwenden.

Mit Grund Nr. 1 das Innere der Puppe
ausfüllen. Den Hintergrund nach Grund
Nr. 3 arbeiten.

DANCING COCKEREL

Bobbins: 5 pairs
Gimps: 1 pair

Work tape A.

DANSENDE HAAN

Klossen: 5 paar
Sierdraden: 1 paar

Klos bandje A.

LE COQ QUI DANSE

Fuseaux: 5 paires
Cordons: 1 paire

Faire la bande A.

TÄNZELDNER HAHN

Klöppel: 5 Paare
Konturfäden: 1 Paar

Band A klöppeln.

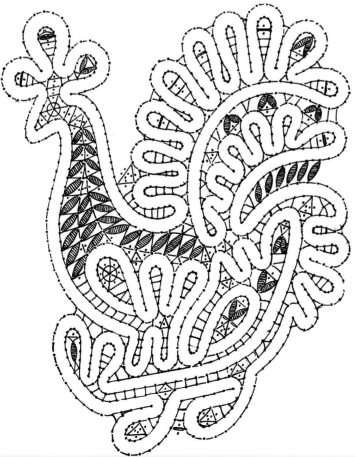

ROCKING HORSE

Bobbins: 5 pairs
Gimps: 1 pair

Work tape B.

HOBBELPAARD

Klossen: 5 paar Sierdraden: 1 paar

Klos bandje B.

CHEVAL A BASCULE

Fuseaux: 5 paires Cordons: 1 paire

Faire la bande B.

SCHAUKELPFERD

Klöppel: 5 Paare Konturfäden: 1 Paar

Band B klöppeln.

VYATSKII TOY

Bobbins: 5 pairs
Gimps: 1 pair

Work tape B for the upper part of the body.
Work tape D for the skirt section.

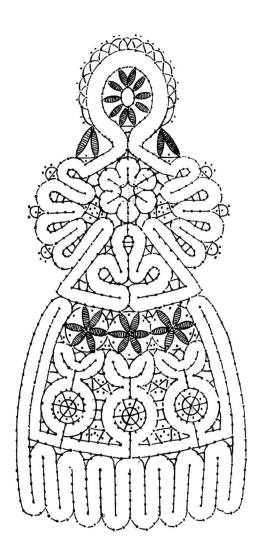

VYATSKII POP

Klossen: 5 paar
Sierdraden: 1 paar

Klos bandje B voor het bovenstuk
van het lijf. Klos bandje D voor het
deel met de rok.

JOUET VYATSKII

Fuseaux: 5 paires
Cordons: 1 paire

Faire la bande B pour la partie
supérieur du corps et la bande D
pour la partie de la jupe.

VYATSKII SPIELZEUG

Klöppel: 5 Paare
Konturfäden: 1 Paar

Das Bad B für den oberen Teil des
Körpers klöppeln. Den Rock mit
Band D arbeiten.

MATRYOSHKA IN OVAL FRAME

Bobbins: 6 pairs
Gimps: 1 pair

Work tape B for both the doll and
frame.

Use background filling note no. 1
as a guide to the threads, and Fig.
1 for help with the route of the
background working.

MATRYOSHKA IN OVALE LIJST

Klossen: 6 paar
Sierdraden: 1 paar

Klos bandje B voor zowel de pop als de lijst.

Gebruik vullingaanwijzing nr. 1 als leidraad
voor de garens, en Fig. 1 als hulp bij de
route voor het werken van de achtergond.

MATRIOSCHKA DANS UN CADRE
OVALE

Fuseaux: 6 paires
Cordons: 1 paire

Faire la bande B pour la poupée et le cadre.
Se reporter au remplissage no. 1 pour le
passage des fils et au dessin 1 pour la
façon de faire le fond.

MATRIOSCHKA IN OVALEM
RAHMEN

Klöppel: 6 Paare
Konturfäden: 1 Paar

Das Band B sowohl für die Puppe
wie für den Rahmen klöppeln. Der
Grund Nr 1 zeigt den Fadenverlauf,
und die Abbildung 1 ist eine Hilfe
für die Füllung des Hintergrundes.

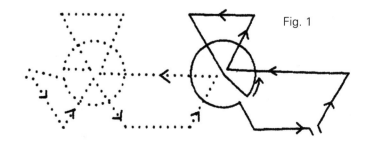

Fig. 1

BROODY COCKEREL

Bobbins: 5 pairs
Gimps: 1 pair for cockerel
         2 pairs for frame

Work tape A for the cockerel and
tape F for the frame.

For the infill of the cockerel use
filling note no. 1.

Background: Filling note no. 3.

SOMBERE HAAN

Klossen: 5 paar
Sierdraden: 1 paar voor de haan
              2 paar voor de lijst

Klos bandje A voor de haan en bandje F
voor de lijst.
Gebruik voor het vullen van de haan
vullingaanwijzing nr. 1.

Achtergrond: vullingaanwijzing nr. 3.

COQ REVEUR

Fuseaux: 5 paires
Cordons: 1 paire pour le coq
          2 paires pour le cadre

Faire la bande A pour le coq et la bande F
pour le cadre.
Pour l'intérieur du coq, voir remplissage
no.1.

Fond: remplissage no. 3.

TRÄUMENDER HAHN

Klöppel: 5 Paare
Konturfäden: 1 Paar für den Hahn
              2 Paare für den Rahmen

Für den Hahn das Band A und für den
Rahmen das Band F klöppeln.
Der Hahn wird mit Grund Nr. 1 ausgefüllt.

Füllung: nach Grund Nr. 3 arbeiten.

LITTLE MAIDEN

Bobbins: 5 pairs
Gimps: 1 pair

Work tape B.
Background: Filling note no. 3.

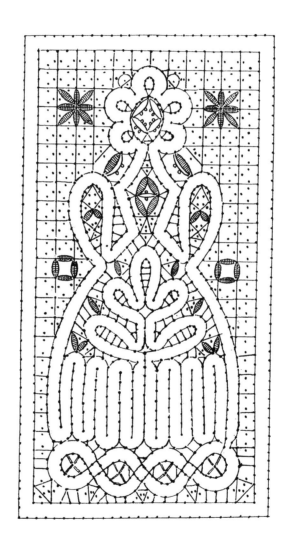

KLEIN MEISJE

Klossen: 5 paar
Siredraden: 1 paar

Klos bandje B
Achtergrond: vullingaanwijzing nr. 3.

FILLETTE

Fuseaux: 5 paires
Cordons: 1 paire

Faire la bande B
Fond: remplissage no. 3.

KLEINES MÄDCHEN

Klöppel: 5 Paare
Konturfäden: 1 Paar

Band B klöppeln.
Grund: Füllung Nr. 3.

BUTTERFLY BLUE

Bobbins: 5 pairs
Gimps: 1 pair

Work tape A.

BLAUWTJE

Klossen: 5 paar
Sierdraden: 1 paar

Klos bandje A.

PAPILLON

Fuseaux: 5 paires
Cordons: 1 paire

Faire la bande A.

SCHMETTERLINGS-KOM-POSITION

Klöppel: 5 Paare
Konturfäden: 1 Paar

Band A klöppeln.

BABY BUTTERFLY

Bobbins: 5 pairs
Gimps: 1 pair

Work tape A.

BABY VLINDER

Klossen: 5 paar
Sierdraden: 1 paar

Klos bandje A.

BEBE PAPILLON

Fuseaux: 5 paires
Cordons: 1 paire

Faire la bande A.

SCHMETTERLINGSBABY

Klöppel: 5 Paare
Konturfäden: 1 Paar

Band A klöppeln.

FROLICKING DEER

Bobbins: 5 pairs
Gimps: 1 pair

Work tape A.

DARTELEND HERT

Klossen: 5 paar
Sierdraden: 1 paar

Klos bandje A.

CERF

Fuseaux: 5 paires
Cordons: 1 paire

Faire la bande A.

SPRINGENDER HIRSCH

Klöppel: 5 Paare
Konturfäden: 1 Paar

Band A klöppeln.

SNOWFLAKES

Bobbins: 6 pairs
Gimps: 1 pair

Work tape A.
See Fig.1 for a guide to working the snowflake filling.
This was made from two plaits. One started from the
inside tape and the other from the outer tape, each
working a complete circle and returning to the start.
The plaits and picot edge are added at the finish.

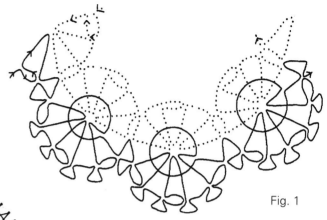

Fig. 1

SNEEUWVLOKKEN

Klossen: 6 paar
Sierdraden: 1 paar

Klos bandje A.

Zie Fig. 1 als leidraad voor het klossen van
de sneeuwvlokvulling. Deze is gemaakt met
twee vlechten. Eén begint bij het binnenste
bandje en de ander bij het buitenste, Beide
vormen een volledige cirkel en eindigen
weer bij het begin.
De vlechten- en de picotrand wordt aan het
eind toegevoegd.

FLOCONS DE NEIGE

Fuseaux: 6 paires
Cordons: 1 paire

Faire la bande A.

Se reporter au dessin 1 pour le remplissage
des flocons. Celui-ci consiste de deux
cordes de 4; l'une commence à la bande
intérieure et l'autre à la bande extérieure,
chacune dessine un cercle complet et
revient au début.
Les cordes de 4 et la bordure de pointons
sont ajoutées à la fin.

SCHNEEFLOCKEN

Klöppel: 6 Paare
Konturfäden: 1 Paar

Band A klöppeln.

Die Abbildung 1 dient als Hilfe für
die Ausfüllung der Schneeflocken.
Dazu werden zwei Flechter geklöppelt.
Einer beginnt am inneren Band und der
andere am äusseren Band, wobei jeder
einen ganzen Kreis bildet und zum
Anfang zurückkehrt.
Die Flechter mit Picot-Umrandung werden
zum Schluss hinzugefügt.

SPICE CAKE

Bobbins: 6 pairs
Gimps: 1 pair

Work tape A.

KRUIDENCAKE

Klossen: 6 paar
Sierdraden: 1 paar

Klos bandje A.

PAIN D'EPICES

Fuseaux: 6 paires
Cordons: 1 paire

Faire la bande A.

GEWÜRZKUCHEN

Klöppel: 6 Paare
Konturfäden: 1 Paar

Band A klöppeln.

ROWAN BERRY

Bobbins: 5 pairs
Gimps: 1 pair

Work tape A.

LIJSTERBES

Klossen: 5 paar
Sierdraden: 1 paar

Klos bandje A.

LA SORBE

Fuseaux: 5 paires
Cordons: 1 paire

Faire la bande A.

VOGELBEERE

Klöppel: 5 Paare
Konturfäden: 1 Paar

Band A klöppeln.

46

LITTLE PEARL

Bobbins: 5 pairs
Gimps: 1 pair

Work tape A.

KLEINE PAREL

Klossen: 5 paar
Sierdraden: 1 paar

Klos bandje A.

PETITE PERLE

Fuseaux: 5 paires
Cordons: 1 paire

Faire la bande A.

KLEINE PERLE

Klöppel: 5 Paare
Konturfäden: 1 Paar

Band A klöppeln.

BERRIES

Bobbins: 6 pairs (cotton)
Gimps: 1 pair

Work tape A.
See Fig.1 as a guide to working the snowflake
background. Note that three short false plaits
will be needed (indicated by dotted lines).

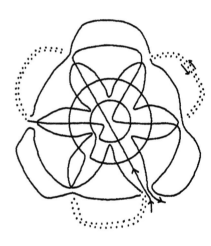

Fig. 1

BESSEN

Klossen: 6 paar (katoen)
Sierdraden: 1 paar

Klos bandje A.

Zie Fig. 1 als leidraad voor het werken van
de sneeuwvlokkenachtergrond. Merk op dat
drie soorten valse vlechten nodig zijn.

LES BAIES

Fuseaux: 6 paires (coton)
Cordons: 1 paire

Faire la bande A.

Les dessin 1 donne des indications
comment travailler le fond à flocons de
neige. A noter que trois fausses cordes
courtes sont nécessaires.

BEEREN

Klöppel: 6 Paare (Baumwolle)
Konturfäden: 1 Paar

Band A klöppeln.

Die Abbildung 1 gibt Hinweise für das
Klöppeln des Schneeflocken-Hintergrundes.
Es ist zu beachten, dass drei kurze falsche
Flechter benötigt werden.

BINDWEED

Bobbins: 5 pairs
Gimps: 1 pair

Work tape F.
The plait picot and leaf border
down either side are worked last.

WINDE

Klossen: 5 paar
Sierdraden: 1 paar

Klos bandje F.
De randen van vlechten, picots en blaadjes
aan beide zijden worden het laatst geklost.

LISERON

Fuseaux: 5 paires
Cordons: 1 paire

Faire la bande F.
Exécuter en dernier la bordure en cordes
de 4, pointons et feuilles descendant de
chaque côté.

ACKERWINDE

Klöppel: 5 Paare
Konturfäden: 1 Paar

Band F klöppeln.
Der Rand mit Flechtern und Picots sowie
die Blätter an beiden Seiten werden
abschliessend gearbeitet.

SUNFLOWER

Bobbins: 5 pairs
Gimps: 1 pair

Work tape B.
Background: Filling note no. 1, for a guide
to the way that the threads are used.

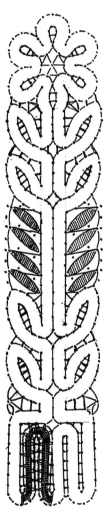

ZONNEBLOEM

Klossen: 5 paar
Sierdraded: 1 paar

Klos bandje B.
Achtergrond: vullingaanwijzing
nr. 1 voor de gebruikte garens.

TOURNESOL

Fuseaux: 5 paires
Cordons: 1 paire

Faire la bande B.
Fond: le remplissage no. 1
montre comment utiliser les fils.

SONNENBLUME

Klöppel: 5 Paare
Konturfäden: 1 Paar

Band B klöppeln.
Grundfüllung: Der Grund
Nr 1 gibt Hinweise, wie die
Fäden verlaufen.

RUNNING RIVER

Bobbins: 5 pairs
Gimps: 1 pair

Work tape G.
Background: Filling note no. 1, for a guide
to the way that the threads are used.

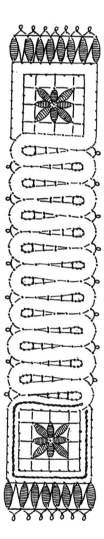

STROMENDE RIVIER

Klossen: 5 paar
Sierdraden: 1 paar

Klos bandje G.
Achtergrond: vullingaanwijzing
nr. 1 als leidraad voor de
gebruikte garens.

EAU VIVE

Fuseaux: 5 paires
Cordons: 1 paire

Faire la bande G.
Fond: le remplissage no. 1 montre
les fils à utiliser.

DER SCHNELLFLIESSENDE
FLUSS

Klöppel: 5 Paare
Konturfäden: 1 Paar

Band G klöppeln.
Füllung: Grund Nr. 1 gibt
Hinweise, wie die Fäden verlaufen.

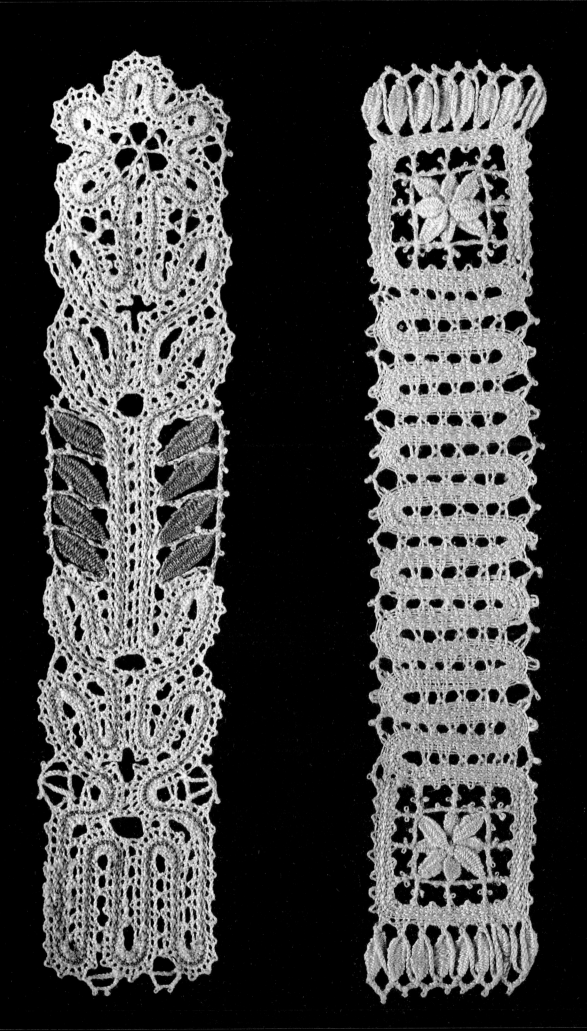

GOLDEN CREEPER

Bobbins: 5 pairs
Gimps: 1 pair

Work tape B.
Background: Filling note no. 1, for a guide
to the way that the threads are used.

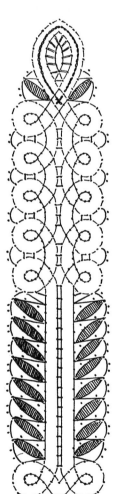

GELE GLIMPLANT

Klossen: 5 paar
Sierdraden: 1 paar

Klos bandje B.
Achtergrond: vullingaanwijzing nr.
1 voor de gebruikte garens.

LIANE D'OR

Fuseaux: 5 paires
Cordons: 1 paire

Faire la bande B.
Fond: le remplissage no. 1 montre
les fils à utiliser.

GOLDLIANE

Klöppel: 5 Paare
Konturfäden: 1 Paar

Band B klöppeln.
Füllung: Grund Nr. 1 gibt
Hinweise, wie die Fäden verlaufen.

SUMMER FRUIT

Bobbins: 5 pairs
Gimps: 1 pair

Work tape B.
Background: Filling note no. 1, for a guide
to the way that the threads are used.

ZOMERFRUIT

Klossen: 5 paar
Sierdraden: 1 paar

Klos banje B.
Achtergrond: vullingaanwijzing
nr. 1 voor de gebruikte garens.

FRUIT D'ETE

Fuseaux: 5 paires
Cordons: 1 paire

Faire la bande B.
Fond: le remplissage no. 1 montre
les fils à utiliser.

SOMMERFRUCHT

Klöppel: 5 Paare
Konturfäden: 1 Paar

Band B klöppeln.
Füllung: Grund Nr. 1.gibt
Hinweise, wie die Fäden verlaufen.

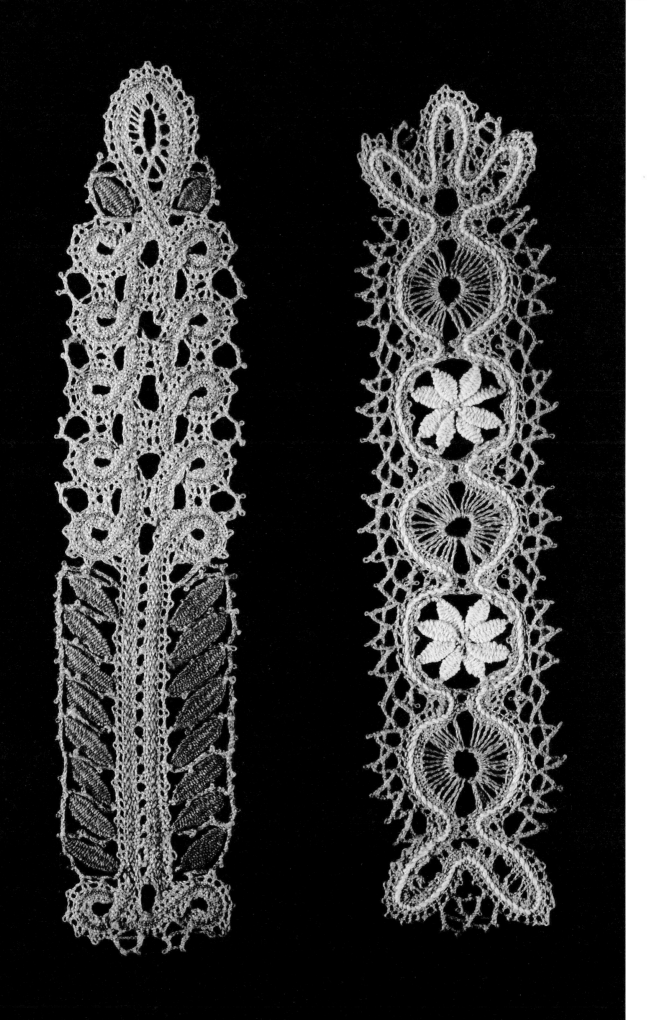

FIRTREE BOW

Bobbins: 6 pairs (cotton)
Gimps: 1 pair

Work tape A.
Background: Filling note no. 2.

SPARRENSTRIK

Klossen: 6 paar
Sierdraden: 1 paar

Klos bandje A.
Achtergrond: vullingaanwijzing nr. 2.

BRANCHE DE SAPIN

Fuseaux: 6 paires
Cordons: 1 paire

Faire la bande A.
Fond: remplissage no. 2.

KIEFERNAST

Klöppel: 6 Paare
Konturfäden: 1 Paar

Band A klöppeln.
Füllung: Grund Nr. 2.

FAN COLLAR

Bobbins: 5 pairs
Gimps: 1 pair

Work as tape F.

WAAIER KRAAG

Klossen: 5 paar
Sierdraden: 1 paar

Klos als bandje F.

COL EVENTAIL

Fuseaux: 5 paires
Cordons: 1 paire

Procéder comme pour la bande F.

FÄCHERKRAGEN

Klöppel: 5 Paare
Konturfäden: 1 Paar

Band F klöppeln.

60

MOON RADIANCE JABOT

Bobbins: 5 pairs
Gimps: 1 pair

Each pair consists of one white and
one black thread. Work as tape A.
Use Fig. 1 as a guide to working
the background.
When working the plaits always
cross the centre threads of matching
colour. This way the plaits are more
attractive. Always use a white thread
to make both the picots and the
leaves. On completion of the
three pieces sew a curved piece
on each side of the straight strip
(Fig. 2). If it is worked this way, it
will fall into graceful folds down
the front of a blouse.

Fig. 1

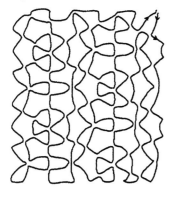

MAANLICHT JABOT

Klossen: 5 paar
Sierdraden: 1 paar

Elk paar bestaat uit een witte en een
swarte draad. Werk als bandje A. Gebruik
Fig. 1 als leidraad voor het klossen van
de achtergrond.
Kruis bij het klossen van de vlechten altijd
de midden draden in deselfde kleur. Op die
manier worden de vlechten mooier. Gebruik
voor zowel picots als blaadjes altijd een witte
draad. Naai bij het afwerken van de drie
stukken altijd een rond stuk aan beide
kanten van de rechte strook. Op deze manier
gemaakt zal de kraag in soepele plooien
over de voorkant van de blouse vallen.

JABOTS RAYONS DE LUNE

Fuseaux: 5 paires
Cordons: 1 paire

Chaque paire est composée d'un fil blanc
et d'un fil noir. Procéder comme pour la
bande A. Le dessin 1 donne des indications
pour faire le fond.
Dans les cordes de 4 croiser toujours les
fils du centre de la même couleur. Ainsi on
obtient un joli résultat. Toujours utiliser
le fil blanc pour les pointons et les feuilles.
Après avoir terminé les trois pièces,
crocheter une partie courbée à chaque
côté du ruban droit. Ainsi le jabot tombera
gracieusement sur le devant du chemisier.

MONDSTRAHLEN-JABOT

Klöppel: 5 Paare
Konturfäden: 1 Paar

Jedes Paar besteht aus einem weissen und
einem schwarzen Faden. Wie bei Band A
vorgehen. Die Abbildung 1 gibt Hinweise,
wie der Hintergrund zu klöppeln ist.
Bei den Flechtern werden stets die
mittleren Fäden derselben Farbe gekreuzt.
So wirken die Flechter besser. Nach
Fertigstellung der drei Teile wird an beiden
Seiten des geraden Streifens ein gebogenes
Teil angehäkelt. Hält man diese Reihenfolge
ein, wird sich das Jabot in gefälligen Falten
auf das Blusenvorderteil legen.

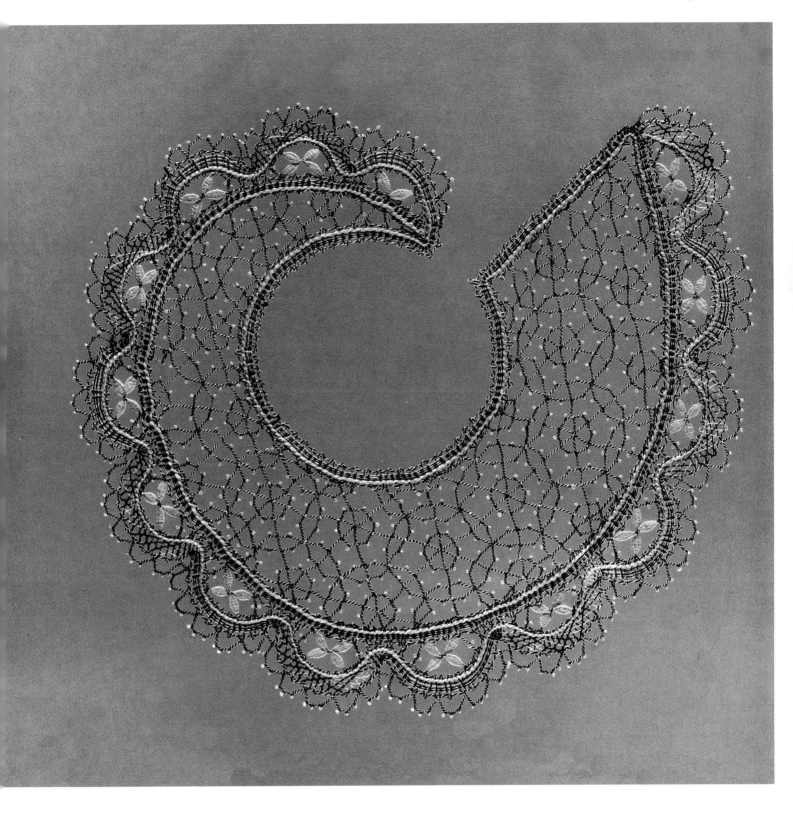

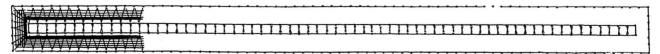

Fig. 2

SPRING MELODIES

Bobbins: 6 pairs
Gimps: 1 pair

Work tape A.

MELODIES DE PRINTEMPS

Fuseaux: 6 paires
Cordons: 1 paire

Faire la bande A.

FRÜHLINGSMELODIEN

Klöppel: 6 Paare
Konturfäden: 1 Paar

Band A klöppeln.

TWO LACEMAKERS

Bobbins: 5 pairs plus 1 extra pair
for frame
Gimps: 1 pair

Work tape G for the lacemakers.
New short tapes are needed in
several places.
Work tape A for the frame,
adding the sixth pair.
Background: Filling note no. 2.

TWEE KANTKLOSSTERS

Klossen: 5 paar plus 1 paar
Sierdraden: 1 paar

Klos bandje G voor de kantklossters. Op
verscheidene plaatsen moeten nieuwe
bandjes worden begonnen.
Klos bandje A voor de lijst, voeg hier het
zesde paar toe.
Achtergrond: vullingaanwijzing nr. 2.

DEUX DENTELLIERES

Fuseaux: 5 paires plus 1 paire
Cordons: 1 paire

Faire les dentellières avec la bande G.
Rajouter des courtes bandes à plusieurs
endroits.
Le cadre se fait avec la bande A et ajoutant
la sixième paire.
Fond: remplissage no. 2.

ZWEI KLÖPPLERINNEN

Klöppel: 5 Paare plus 1 Paar
Konturfäden: 1 Paar

Für die Klöpplerinnen Band G klöppeln.
An mehreren Stellen benötigt man neue
kurze Bänder. Den Rahmen mit Band A
anfertigen, nachdem ein 6. Paar
hinzugefügt wurde.
Füllung: Grund Nr. 2.

RUSSIAN SARAFHAN

Bobbins: 6 pairs plus 2 single silver threads
Gimps: 2 pairs

Each silver thread is worked with a black thread as
a pair. These pairs are worked in clothstitch on either
side of the central passives, placing the black thread
on the outer edge and then the silver.
Work tape F.

RUSSISCHE SARAFAAN

Klossen: 6 paar plus 2 enkele
zilverdraden
Sierdraden 2 paar

Elke zilverdraad wordt met een
zwarte draad samen gewerkt als
een paar. Deze paren worden in
linnenslag geklost aan beide zijden
van de middelste hangende paren,
waarbij de zwarte draad aan de
buitenkant ligt en daarnaast
de zilveren.
Klos bandje F.

EMPIECEMENT RUSSE

Fuseaux: 6 paires plus 2 fils d'argent
séparés
Cordons: 2 paires

Chaque fil d'argent est utilisé
ensemble avec un fil noir pour faire
une paire. Ces paires travaillent en
mat de chaque côté des paires passives
centrales, le fil noir se trouvant au
bord extérieur suivi du fil argent.
Faire la bande F.

RUSSISCHER EINSATZ

Klöppel: 6 Paare und 2 einzelne
Silberfäden
Konturfäden: 2 Paare

Jeder Silberfaden wird mit einem
schwarzen Faden als Paar verarbeitet.
Diese Paare werden an beiden
Seiten der mittleren Risspaare im
Leinenschlag geklöppelt, wobei der
schwarze Faden am äusseren Rand
vor dem Silberfaden verläuft.
Band F klöppeln.

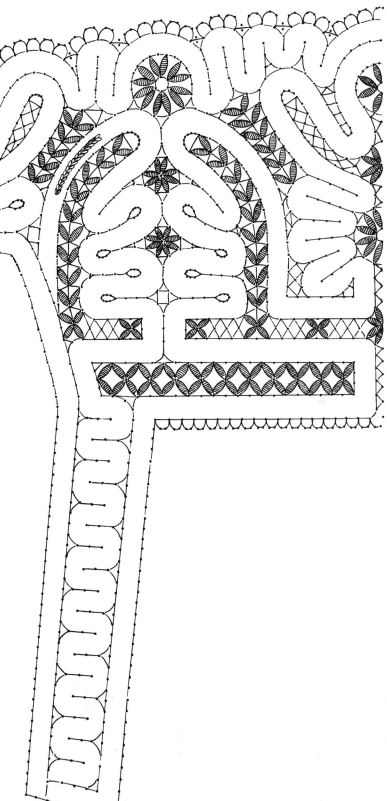

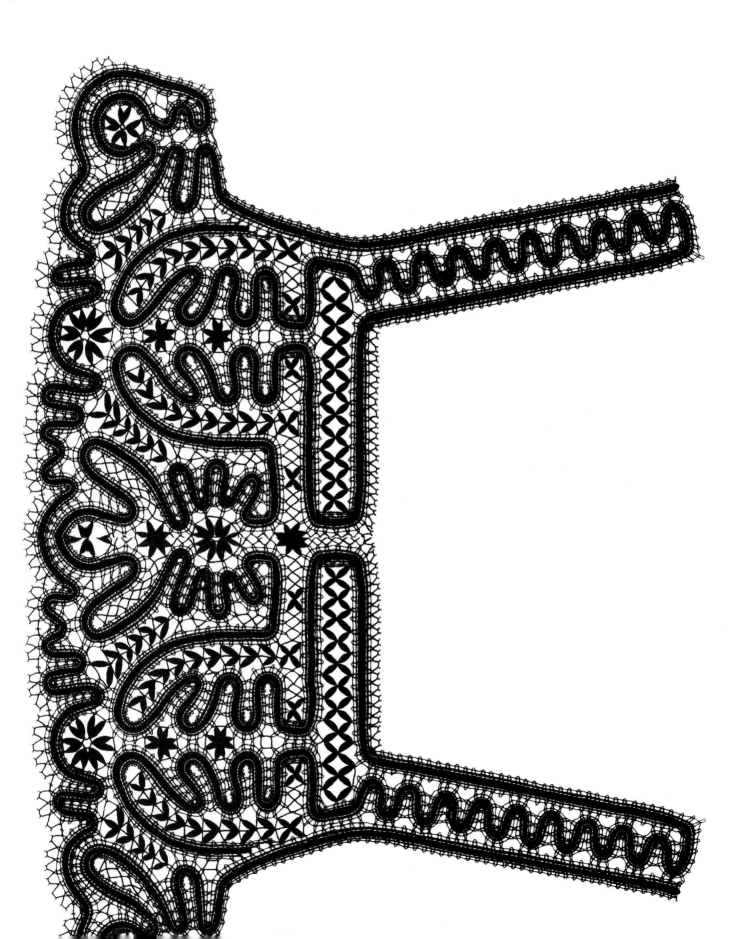

VOLOGDA DRESS FRONT

Bobbins: 5 pairs (cotton) plus 1 pair with 1 silver and 1 cotton thread
Gimps: 1 pair

Work tape A.
The silver/cotton pair is worked adjacent to the gimp pair. This pair is clothstitched throughout. Place the cotton thread next to the gimp pair and then the silver.

JAPONFRONT UIT VOLOGDA

Klossen: 5 paar katoen, plus 1 paar met 1 zilver- en 1 katoenen draad
Sierdraden: 1 paar

Klos bandje A.
Het zilver/katoenen paar wordt naast het sierdraadpaar geklost. Dit paar wordt voortdurend in linnenslag gewerkt. Leg de katoenen draad naast het sierdraadpaar en daarnaast de zilveren.

DEVANT DE ROBE DE VOLOGDA

Fuseaux: 5 paires (coton) plus 1 paire composée d'un fil argent et d'un fil coton.
Cordons: 1 paire

Faire la bande A.
La paire en argent/coton est travaillée à côté de la paire des cordons et mat, le fil coton étant le plus proche de la paire des cordons, suivi du fil d'argent.

KLEIDERPLASTRON VON VOLGDA

Klöppel: 5 Paare (Baumwolle) und 1 Paar mit je einem Silber-und einem Baumwollfaden.
Konturfäden: 1 Paar

Band A klöppeln.
Das Silber-Baumwollpaar wird neben dem Konturfadenpaar geklöppelt, und zwar stets im Leinenschlag. Der Baumwollfaden liegt direkt neben dem Konturfadenpaar, dann kommt der Silberfaden.

SAILOR COLLAR

Bobbins: 6 pairs
Gimps: 1 pair

The twisted gimp lies in the second position
of the central passives towards the outer edge.
Use Fig. 1 for help with the route of the
background working.

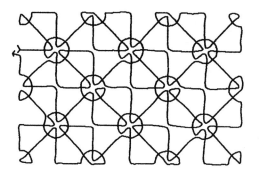

Fig. 1

MATROZENKRAAG

Klossen: 6 paar
Sierdraden: 1 paar

De gedraaide seirdraad ligt op de tweede
plaats tussen de middelste hangende paren
naar de buitenrand toe.
Gebruik Fig. 1 als hulp voor de werkrichting
bij het klossen van de achtergrond.

COL MARIN

Fuseaux: 6 paires
Cordons: 1 paire

Les cordons tordus se trouvent en deuxième
position des paires centrales passives vers le
bord entérieur.
Le dessin 1 donne des indications pour le
travail du fond.

SEEMANNSKRAGEN

Klöppel: 6 Paare
Konturfäden: 1 Paar

Die gedrehten Konturfäden verlaufen in
zweiter Position der mittleren Risspaare
zum äusseren Rand hin.
Die Abbildung 1 gibt Hinweise über die
Arbeitsweise der Füllung.

MASHENKA

Bobbins: 6 pairs
Gimps: 1 pair plus
1 single silver thread

Work tape A.
The twisted gimp pair and the
single thread are worked together;
one of the gimp threads and the
silver thread work as a single
thread, twisted slightly so that
they appear to be one thread.
This adds sparkle to the collar.

MASHENKA

Klossen: 6 paar
Sierdraden: 1 paar plus 1 enkele zilverdraad

Het gedraaide sierdraadpaar en de enkele
draad worden samen gewerkt; één van de
sierdraden werkt samen met de zilverdraad
als een enkele draad, licht gedraaid zodat
ze één draad lijken te zijn. Dit geeft de
kraag iets sprankelends.
Klos bandje A.

MASHENKA

Fuseaux: 6 paires
Cordons: 1 paire plus un seul fil argent

La paire de cordons tordus et le fil argent
sont travaillés ensemble. Un fil des cordons
est tordu légèrement avec le fil argent pour
former un seul fil. Ceci donne du brillant
au col.
Faire la bande A.

KRAGEN MASCHENKA

Klöppel: 6 Paare
Konturfäden: 1 Paar und ein einzelner
Silberfaden

Das gedrehte Konturfadenpaar wird mit
dem Einzelfaden zusammen geklöppelt;
einer der Konturfäden und der Silberfaden
werden wie ein einziger Faden behandelt
und leicht miteinander gedreht, so dass
sie ein einziger Faden zu sein scheinen.
Dadurch wirkt der Kragen glänzender.
Band A klöppeln.

BLOSSOM COLLAR

Bobbins: 6 pairs
Gimps: 1 pair

Work tape A.
On the outer edge two pins are used for each point: one on the edge of the twisted clothstitch line (inner pin holes) and one for each point. More twists are needed on the worker pair so that these points are held firm for wear and tear.

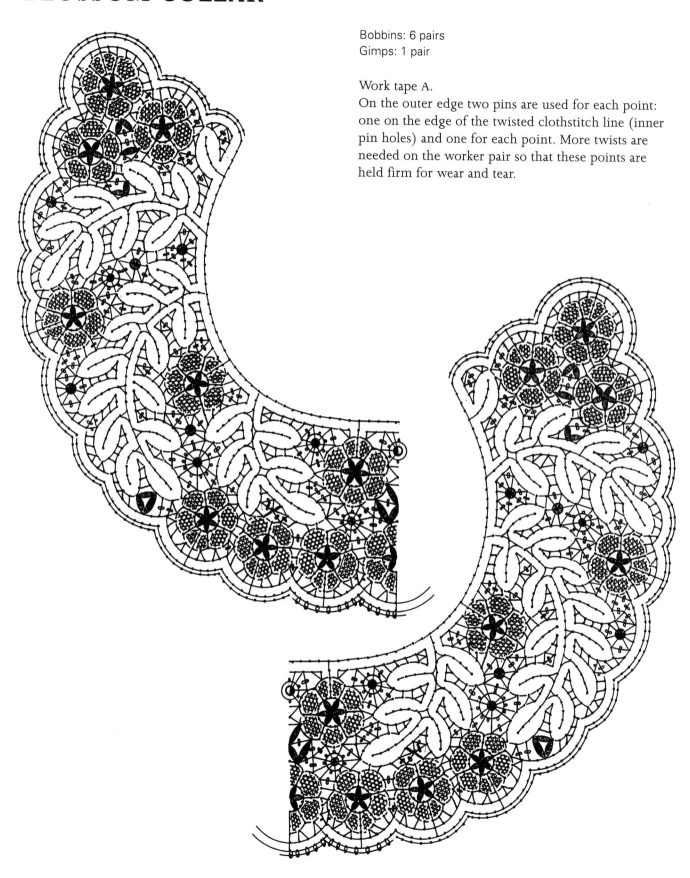

BLOESEMKRAAG

Klossen: 6 paar
Sierdraden: 1 paar

Werk banje A.
Aan de buitenrand worden voor elke punt
twee spelden gebruikt: één op de rand van
de netslaglijn (binnenste speldepunten) en
één voor elke punt. Op het looppaar zijn
meer draaiïngen nodig opdat deze punten
stevig blijven tijdens het gebruik.

COL A FLEURS

Fuseaux: 6 paires
Cordons: 1 paire

Faire la bande A.
Sur le bord extérieur utiliser deux épingles
pour chaque point: une en bordure de la
ligne de grille (trous d'épingles intérieurs)
et une pour chaque point. Ajouter des
torsions à la paire des meneurs pour
rendre ces points plus solides.

BLÜTENKRAGEN

Klöppel: 6 Paare
Konturfäden: 1 Paar

Band A klöppeln.
Am äusseren Rand werden für jeden Punkt
zwei Nadeln verwendet: eine am Rand der
Netzschlaglinie (innere Nadellöcher) und
eine für jeden Punkt. Das Laufpaar ist
mehrere Male zu drehen, damit diese
Punkte solide sind und jeder
Beanspruchung widerstehen.

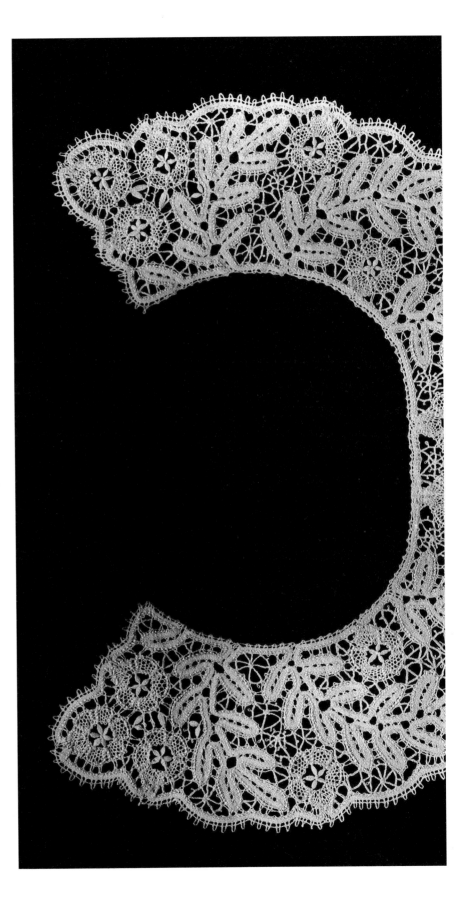

DAWN BLOSSOM

Bobbins: 7 pairs
Gimps: 1 pair

Work tape A.
For a guide to the background see Fig. 1.

Fig. 1

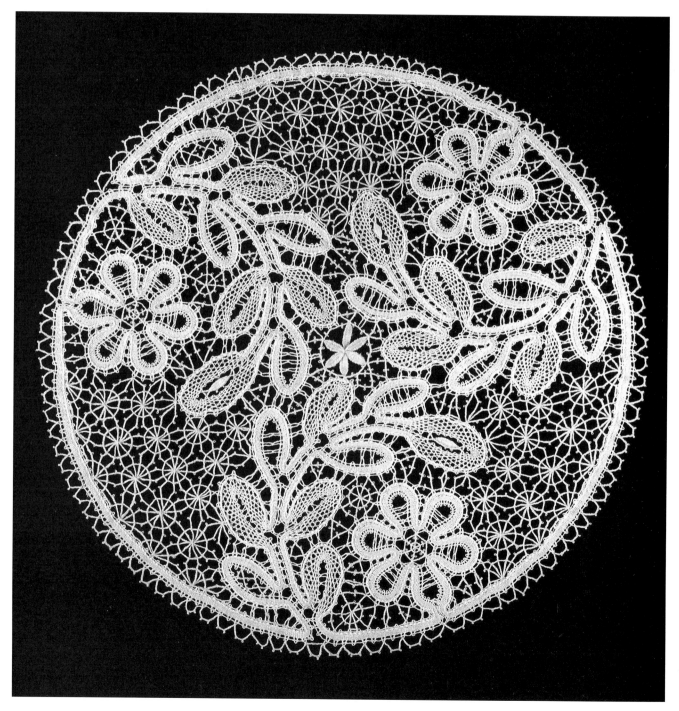

MORGENBLOESEM

Klossen: 7 paar
Sierdraden: 1 paar

Klos bandje A.
Zie Fig. 1 voor hulp bij de achtergrond.

AURORE

Fuseaux: 7 paires
Cordons: 1 paire

Faire la bande A.
Le dessin 1 donne des indications pour le travail du fond.

DÄMMERUNGSBLÜTE

Klöppel: 7 Paare
Konturfäden: 1 Paar

Band A klöppeln.
Bei der Ausführung des Hintergrundes hilft Abbildung 1.

FROST

Bobbins: 5 pairs
Gimps: 1 pair

Work tape F.

VORST

Klossen: 5 paar
Sierdraden: 1 paar

Klos bandje F.

GEL

Fuseaux: 5 paires
Cordons: 1 paire

Faire la bande F.

FROST

Klöppel: 5 Paare
Konturfäden: 1 Paar

Band F klöppeln.

GEMS

Bobbins: 5 pairs plus 1 mixed pair
with 1 silver and 1 linen thread
Gimps: 1 pair

Work tape A with the mixed pair
next to the gimp pair.
For the fan edge use three pairs
plus one mixed pair and one
gimp pair. Work as tape D.

EDELSTENEN

Klossen: 5 paar plus 1 gemengd paar met 1
zilveren en 1 linnen draad
Sierdrade: 1 paar

Werk bandje A met het gemengde paar
naast het sierdraadpaar.
Gebruik voor de waaierrand drie paar plus
één gemengd paar en één sierdraadpaar.
Klos als bandje D.

PIERRES PRECIEUSES

Fuseaux: 5 paires plus une paire composée
d'un fil argent et d'un fil de lin
Cordons: 1 paire

Faire la bande A, la paire mélangée étant
utilisée à côté de la paire des cordons.
Pour le bord à coquilles, travailler avec
trois paires plus une paire mélangée et
une paire de cordons. Porcéder comme
pour la bande D.

EDELSTEINE

Klöppel: 5 Paare und ein gemischtes Paar
aus 1 Silber- und Leinenfaden
Konturfäden: 1 Paar

Band A klöppeln, wobei das gemischte
Paar neben dem Konturfadenpaar liegt.
Für den Fächerrand braucht man drei
Paare, sowie ein gemischtes und ein
Konturfadenpaar. Wie Band D klöppeln.

BELL CHIMES

Fig. 1

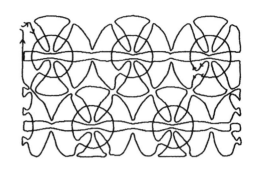

Bobbins: 7 pairs
Gimps: 1 pair

Work tape A.
For a guide to the background see Fig. 1.

KLOKGELUI

Klossen: 7 paar
Sierdraden: 1 paar

Klos bandje A.
Gebruik Fig. 1 als leidraad bij de
achtergrond.

CARILLON

Fuseaux: 7 paires
Cordons: 1 paire

Faire la bande A.
Le dessin 1 donne des indications
pour le travail du fond.

GLOCKENSPIEL

Klöppel: 7 Paare
Konturfäden: 1 Paar

Band A klöppeln.
Die Abbildung 1 gibt Hinweise für
die Ausführung des Hintergrundes.

FERTILITY PANEL

Bobbins: 4 pairs plus 1 pair with one matching thread
and the other a thread of a contrasting colour. Work as
a mixed pair
Gimps: 1 pair

Work tape A using the mixed pair on the outer edge
so that the fillings can be worked with this pair and
the worker pair.
Background: Filling note no. 3.

VRUCHTBAARHEIDSWAND-KLEED

Klossen: 4 paar en 1 paar met één draad
in dezelfde kleur en één draad in een
contrasterende kleur. Werk ze als een
gemengd paar.
Sierdraden: 1 paar

Klos bandje A met het gemengde paar
aan de buitenrand, zodat de vullingen
geklost kunnen worden met dit paar
en het looppaar.
Achtergrond: vullingaanwijzing nr. 3.

PANNEAU FECONDITE

Fuseaux: 4 paires plus 1 paire composée
d'un fil identique et d'un fil d'une couleur
contrastante. Travailler les deux fils
ensemble comme paire mélangée.
Cordons: 1 paire

Faire la bande A en utilisant la paire
mélangée sur le bord extérieur pour
pouvoir la prendre ensemble avec les
meneurs pour faire le remplissage.
Fond: remplissage no. 3.

FRUCHTBARKEITSBILD

Klöppel: 4 Paare und 1 Paar mit einem
gleichen und einem kontrastierenden
Faden. Beide Fäden als gemischtes
Paar verarbeiten.
Konturfäden: 1 Paar

Das Band A mit dem gemischten Paar
am äusseren Rand klöppeln, so dass die
Füllungen mit dem gemischten und dem
Laufpaar geklöppelt werden können.
Füllung. Grund Nr. 3.

SNOW MAIDEN

Bobbins: 6 pairs
Gimps: 1 pair

Work as tape A but place the gimp pair in
the second position of the central passives.
Background: Filling note no. 3.

SNEEUWMEISJE

Klossen: 6 paar
Sierdraden: 1 paar

Klos als Bandje A, maar leg het sierdraadpaar op de tweede plaats in de middelste
hangende paren.
Achtergrond: vullingaanwijzing nr. 3.

FILLE DES NEIGES

Fuseaux: 6 paires
Cordons: 1 paire

Procéder comme pour la bande A, mais en
plaçant la paire des cordons en deuxième
position des paires centrales passives.
Fond: remplissage no. 3.

SCHNEEMÄDCHEN

Klöppel: 6 Paare
Konturfäden: 1 Paar

Wie Band A verfahren, jedoch das
Konturfadenpaar in zweiter Position
der mittleren Risspaare anordnen.
Füllung: Grund Nr. 3.

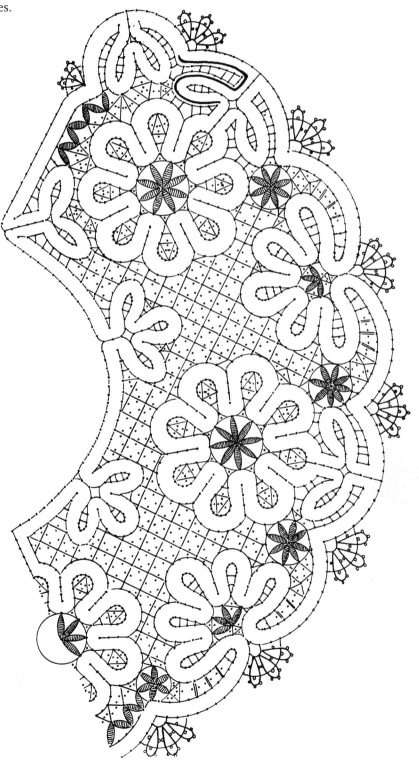

VASSILISSA: THE BEAUTIFUL

Bobbins: 6 pairs
Gimps: 2 pairs

Work tape E. When the tape opens out in a
figure-eight trail, work as tape D.
For the background guide see Figs. 1 and 2.

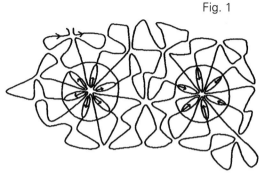

Fig. 1

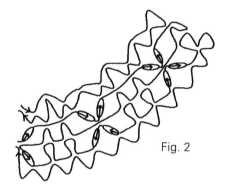

Fig. 2

VASSILISSA: DE SCHONE

Klossen: 6 paar
Sierdraden: 2 paar

Werk bandje E. Waar het bandje zich
splitst en overgaat in een achtvormige
band, klossen als bandje D.
Voor de achtergrong zie Fig. 1 en 2.

LE BEAU VASSILISSA

Fuseaux: 6 paires
Cordons: 2 paires

Faire la bande E. A l'endroit où la bande
s'élargit pour former un huit, procéder
comme pour la bande D.
Les dessins 1 et 2 donnent des indications
concernant le fond.

DER SCHÖNE VASSILISSA

Klöppel: 6 Paare
Konturfäden: 2 Paare

Das Band E klöppeln. Dort wo das Band
sich zu einer Achterfigur erweitert, wie
Band D verfahren. Für den Grund die
Abbildungen 1 und 2 beachten.

FIREBIRD

Bobbins: 7 pairs
Gimps: 1 pair

Work tape C.
For the background guide see Fig. 1.

Fig. 1

VUURVOGEL

Klossen: 7 paar
Sierdraden: 1 paar

Klos bandje C.
Voor de achtergrond zie
Fig. 1.

OISEAU DE FEU

Fuseaux: 7 paires
Cordons: 1 paire

Faire la bande C.
Le dessin 1 donne des indications concernant le fond.

FEUERVOGEL

Klöppel: 7 Paare
Konturfäden: 1 Paar

Das Band C klöppeln.
Für den Grund die
Abbildung 1 beachten.

BIRD GLEAMS

Bobbins: 7 pairs
Gimps: 1 pair

Work tape C.
For the background guide see Figs. 1 and 2.

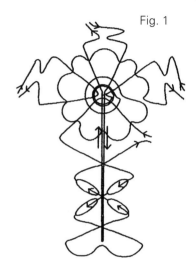

Fig. 1

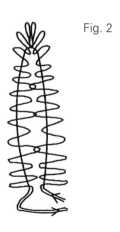

Fig. 2

VOGELSTRALEN

Klossen: 7 paar
Sierdraden: 1 paar

Klos bandje C.
Zie voor de achtergrond Fig. 1 en 2.

OISEAUX DE PARADIS

Fuseaux: 7 paires
Cordons: 1 paire

Faire la bande C.
Les dessins 1 et 2 donnent des indications
concernant le fond.

VOGELPRACHT

Klöppel: 7 Paare
Konturfäden: 1 Paar

Das Band C klöppeln.
Für den Grund Abbildungen
1 und 2 beachten.

APPLE BLOSSOM

Bobbins: 6 pairs
Gimps: 1 pair

Work tape C.

APPELBLOESEM

Klossen: 6 paar
Sierdraden: 1 paar

Klos bandje C.

FLEUR DE POMMIER

Fuseaux: 6 paires
Cordons: 1 paire

Faire la bande C.

APFELBLÜTE

Klöppel: 6 Paare
Konturfäden: 1 Paar

Das Band C klöppeln.

SUMMER

Bobbins: 6 pairs
Gimps: 1 pair

Work tape A.

ZOMER	**ETE**	**SOMMER**
Klossen: 6 paar	Fuseaux: 6 paires	Klöppel: 6 Paare
Sierdraden: 1 paar	Cordons: 1 paire	Konturfäden: 1 Paar
Werk bandje A.	Faire la bande A.	Band A klöppeln.

DIAMOND

Bobbins: 5 pairs
Gimps: 2 pairs

Work tape F.
Background:
Filling note no. 3.

RUIT

Klossel: 5 paar
Sierdraden: 2 paar

Klos bandje F.
Achtergrond: vullingaanwijzing nr. 3.

DIAMANT

Fuseaux: 5 paires
Cordons: 2 paires

Faire la bande F.
Fond: remplissage no. 3.

DIAMANT

Klöppel: 5 Paare
Konturfäden: 2 Paare

Band F klöppeln.
Füllung: Grund Nr. 3.

TRADITIONAL MATRYOSHKA

Bobbins: Various numbers of
bobbins are used in each section

This doll is worked so that the
threads sit tightly together. The
lacemaker must decide the number
of pairs that will be needed for
each part. Work tapes as tape A.

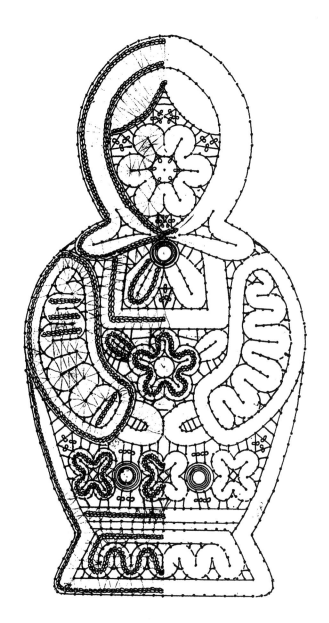

TRADITIONELE MATRYOSHKA

Klossen: in de verschillende onderdelen
is een varierend aantal klossen gebruikt.

Deze pop is zo gemaakt dat de draden dicht
tegen elkaar aan liggen. De kantwerk(-st)er
moet zelf beslissen hoeveel paar nogid zijn
voor elk deel.
Klos de bandjes als bande A.

MATRIOSCHKA TRADITIONELLE

Fuseaux: Un nombre variable de fuseaux
est utilisé dans chaque partie.

La poupée a été faite de façon que les
fils soient serrés. Le nombre de paires
nécessaires pour chaque partie est laissé
à l'appréciation de la dentellière. Les
bandes se font comme la bande A.

TRADITIONELLE MATRIOSCHKA

Klöppel: In jedem Abschnitt wird mit einer
anderen Anzahl von Klöppel gearbeitet.

Diese Puppe wird so geklöppelt, dass
die Fäden dicht nebeneinander liegen.
Die Klöpplerin muss selbst entscheiden,
wieviele Paare sie für jeden Abschnitt
benötigt. Die Bänder sind wie Band A
zu klöppeln.

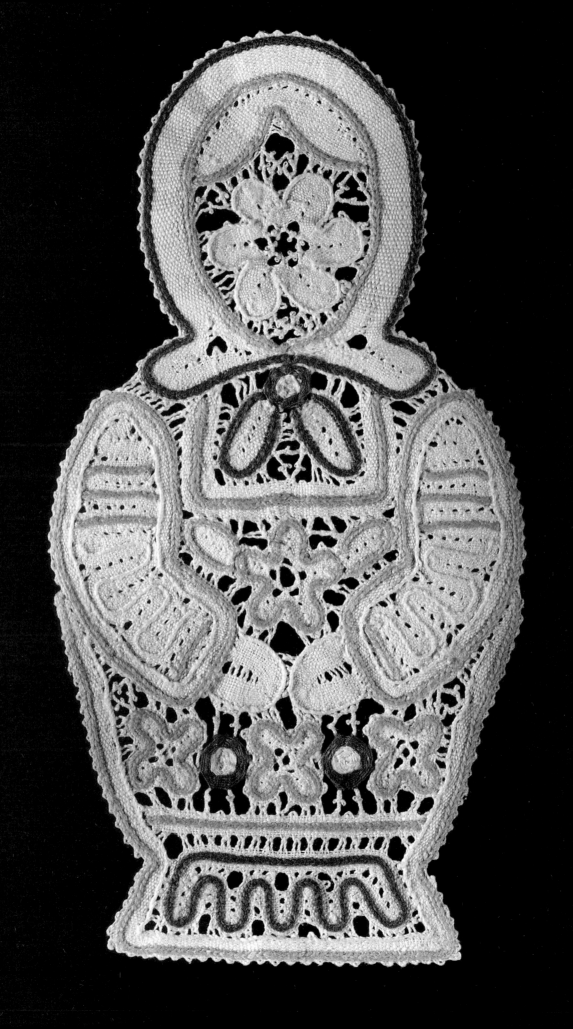

WELCOME! BREAD AND SALT

Bobbins: 6 pairs
Gimps: 1 pair

Work tape G.
Background: Filling note no. 3.
The letters are put in at the end with
two pairs of contrasting colour. These
can be omitted if desired.

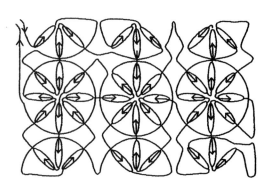

WELKOM! BROOD EN ZOUT

Klossen: 6 paar
Sierdraden: 1 paar

Klos bandje G.
Achtergrond: vullingaanwijzing nr. 3.
De letters worden er het laatst in gemaakt
met twee paar in een contrasterende
kleur. Ze kunnen, indien gewenst,
weggelaten worden.

BIENVENUE! PAIN ET SEL

Fuseaux: 6 paires
Cordons: 1 paire

Faire la bande G.
Fond: remplissage no. 3.
Les lettres sont ajoutées à la fin avec deux
paires de couleur opposée; elles peuvent
être omises.

WILLKOMMEN! BROT UND SALZ

Klöppel: 6 Paare
Konturfäden: 1 Paar

Band G klöppeln.
Füllung: Grund Nr. 3.
Die Buchstaben werden abschliessend mit
zwei Paaren in einer kontrastierenden Farbe
eingefügt. Falls gewünscht, können sie
auch weggelassen werden.

CAMOMILE

Bobbins: 5 pairs
Gimps: 1 pair

Work tape A.
For the background
guide see Fig. 1.

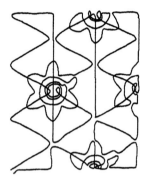

Fig. 1

KAMILLE

Klossen: 5 paar
Sierdraden: 1 paar

Klos bandje A.
Zie voor de achtergrond Fig. 1.

CAMOMILLE

Fuseaux: 5 paires
Cordons: 1 paire

Faire la bande A.
Le dessin 1 donne des indications
pour le fond.

KAMILLE

Klöppel: 5 Paare
Konturfäden: 1 Paar

Band A klöppeln.
Für dem Grund gibt Abbildung 1 Hinweise.

BLUEBELLS

Bobbins: 5 pairs
Gimps: 1 pair

Work as tape A.
For the background
guide see Fig. 1.

Fig. 1

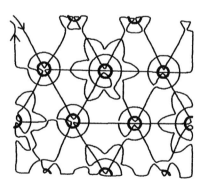

CAMPANULAS

Klossen: 5 paar
Sierdraden: 1 paar

Klos als bandje A.
Voor de achtergrond, zie Fig. 1.

CAMPANULE

Fuseaux: 5 paires
Cordons: 1 paire

Procéder comme pour la bande A. Le dessin
1 donne des indications pour le fond.

GLOCKENBLUME

Klöppel: 5 Paare
Konturfäden: 1 Paar

Wie Band A anfertigen.
Für dem Grund gibt Abbildung 1 Hinweise.

SUMMER BLOOMS

Bobbins: 5 pairs
Gimps: 1 pair

Work tape A.
Background:
Filling note no. 2.

HOOGZOMER

Klossen: 5 paar
Sierdraden: 1 paar

Klos bandje A
Achtergrond: vullingaanwijzing nr. 2.

FLEURS D'ETE

Fuseaux: 5 paires
Cordons: 1 paire

Faire la bande A
Fond: remplissage no. 2.

SOMMERBLUMEN

Klöppel: 5 Paare
Konturfäden: 1 Paar

Band A klöppeln.
Füllung: Grund Nr. 2.

WINTER FROST

Bobbins: 6 pairs
Gimps: 1 pair

Work tape A.

WINTERKOU

Klossen: 6 paar
Sierdraden: 1 paar

Klos bandje A.

GIVRE

Fuseaux: 6 paires
Cordons: 1 paire

Faire la bande A.

WINTERFROST

Klöppel: 6 Paare
Konturfäden: 1 Paar

Band A klöppeln.

RUSSIAN BEAUTY

Bobbins: 5 pairs
Gimps: 1 pair

Work as tape A.
Background: Filling
note no. 3.

RUSSISCHE SCHOONHEID

Klossen: 5 paar
Sierdraden: 1 paar

Werk als bandje A.
Achtergrond: vullingaanwijzing nr. 3.

BEAUTE RUSSE

Fuseaux: 5 paires
Cordons: 1 paire

Procéder comme pour la bande A.
Fond: remplissage no. 3.

RUSSISCHE SCHÖNHEIT

Klöppel: 5 Paare
Konturfäden: 1 Paar

Wie Band A klöppeln.
Füllung: Grund Nr. 3.

RUSSIAN BEAUTY continued/aanhoudend/suite/fortsetzung

BREATH OF SPRING PANEL

Bobbins: 5 pairs Gimps: 1 pair

Work tape A.
The panel is made in three parts. Work tape A. Use tape A for
the surrounding frame as well. The parts are then connected
with a plait and leaf filling, worked as filling note no. 2.

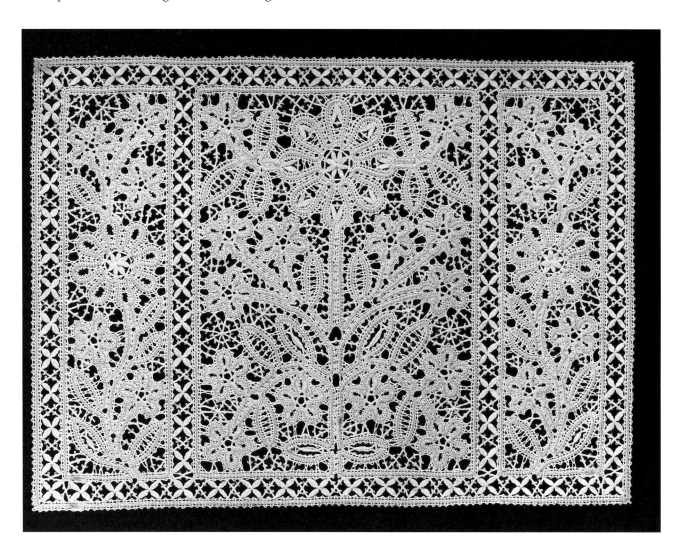

WANDKLEED LENTEBRIES

Klossen: 5 paar
Sierdraden: 1 paar

Klos bandje A.
Het wandkleed wordt in drie delen
gemaakt. Klos bandje A. Gebruik bandje A
ook voor de omlijsting. Daarna worden de
delen verbonden met een vulling van
vlechten en blaadjes, geklost volgens
vullingaanwijzing nr. 2.

PANNEAU AIR DE PRINTEMPS

Fuseaux: 5 paires
Cordons: 1 paire

Faire la bande A.
Le panneau se fait en trois parties. La bande
A est également utilisée pour l'encadrage.
Les parties sont reliées avec un remplissage
de cordes de 4 et de feuilles, exécuté selon
le remplissage no. 2.

WANDBILD FRÜHLINGSLUFT

Klöppel: 5 Paare
Konturfäden: 1 Paar

Der Behang ist in drei Teilen ausgeführt.
Band A klöppeln, und dies auch für
den Rahmen. Die Teile werden
anschliessend mit einem Grund aus
Flechtern und Blättern gemäss Grund
Nr. 2 zusammengefügt.

VOLOGODSKII SUNSET

Fig. 1

Bobbins: 6 pairs
Gimps: 1 pair

Work tape A.
For the background edge guide
see Fig. 1.

ZONSONDERGANG IN VOLOGDA

Klossen: 6 paar
Sierdraden: 1 paar

Klos bandje A.
Zie voor de rand in achtergrondpatroon,
Fig. 1.

COUCHER DE SOLEIL A VOLOGDA

Fuseaux: 6 paires
Cordons: 1 paire

Faire la bande A.
Pour l'angle du fond suivre les indications
du dessin 1.

SONNENUNTERGANG IN VOLOGDA

Klöppel: 6 Paare
Konturfäden: 1 Paar

Band A klöppeln.
Für die Ecke des Hintergrunds siehe
Abbildung 1.

NORTHERN LIGHTS

Bobbins: 6 pairs
Gimps: 1 pair

Work tape A.

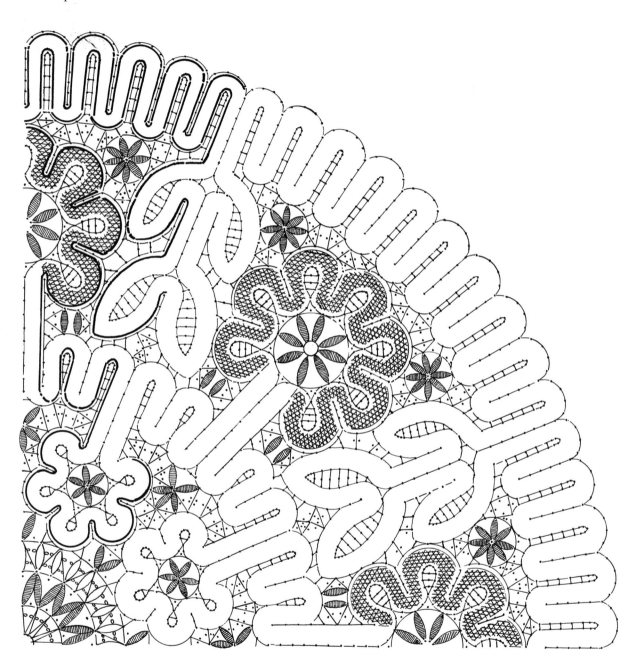

NOODERLICHT

Klossen: 6 paar
Sierdraden: 1 paar

Klos bandje A.

AURORE BOREALE

Fuseaux: 6 paires
Cordons: 1 paire

Faire la bande A.

NORDLICHTER

Klöppel: 6 Paare
Konturfäden: 1 Paar

Band A klöppeln.

VOLOGODSKII FLOWER COLLAR

Bobbins: 5 pairs in cotton
Gimps: 1 pair

Work tape A.

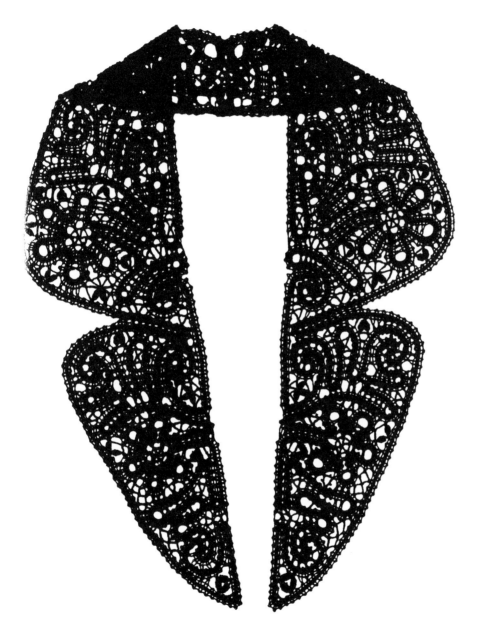

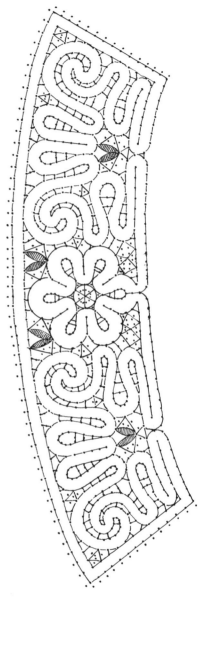

BLOEMENKRAAG UIT VOLOGDA

Klossen: 5 paar katoen
Sierdraden: 1 paar

Klos bandje A.

COL FLEURI DE VOLOGDA

Fuseaux: 5 paires en coton
Cordons: 1 paire

Faire la bande A.

BLUMENKRAGEN VON VOLOGDA

Klöppel: 5 Paare Baumwolle
Konturfäden: 1 Paar

Band A klöppeln.

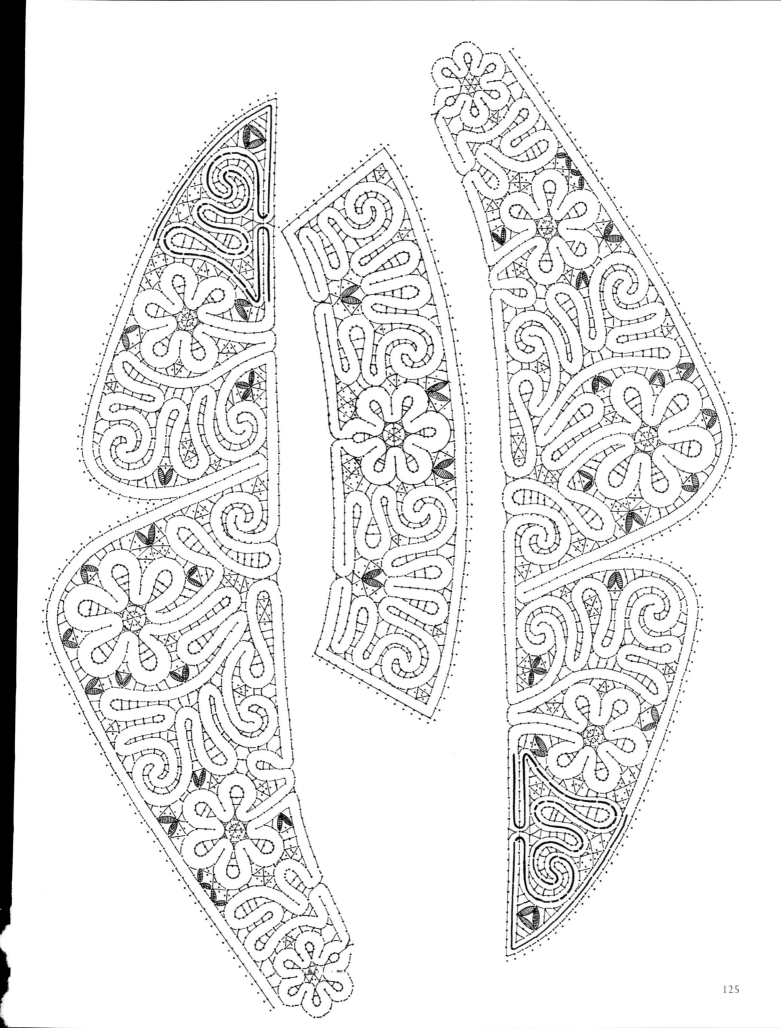

125

ROSES

Bobbins: 5 pairs
Gimps: 1 pair

Work tape A.
Background:
Filling note no. 2.

ROZEN

Klossen: 5 paar
Sierdraden: 1 paar

Klos bandje A.
Achtergrond: vullingaanwijzing nr. 2.

ROSES

Fuseaux: 5 paires
Cordons: 1 paire

Faire la bande A.
Fond: remplissage no. 2.

ROSEN

Klöppel: 5 Paare
Konturfäden: 1 Paar

Band A klöppeln,
Füllung: Grund Nr. 2.

126

CHRYSANTHEMUMS

Bobbins: 6 pairs
Gimps: 1 pair

Work tape A.
For the background
guide see Fig. 1.

Fig. 1

CHRYSANTHEN

Klossen: 6 paar
Sierdraden: 1 paar

Klos bandje A
Zie voor de achtergrond Fig. 1.

CHRYSANTHEME

Fuseaux: 6 paires
Cordons: 1 paire

Faire la bande A.
Le dessin 1 indique comment faire le fond.

CHRYSANTHEME

Klöppel: 6 Paare
Konturfäden: 1 Paar

Band A klöppeln. Die Abbildung 1 gibt
Hinweise für den Grund.

BURDOCK

Bobbins: 5 pairs plus
1 extra pair for frame
Gimps: 1 pair

For the centre
panel use five pairs
and work tape C.
Add the extra pair
for the frame still
working as tape C.
Background:
Filling note no. 2.

KLIS

Klossen: 5 paare plus 1 paar
Sierdraden: 1 paar

Gebruik voor het middenstuk vijf paar en
klos bandje C.
Voeg voor de omlijsting het extra paar toe
en blijf klossen als bandje C.
Achtergrond: vullingaanwijzing nr. 2.

BARDANE

Fuseaux: 5 paires plus 1 paire
Cordons: 1 paire

Pour le panneau central prendre cinq
paires et faire la bande C. Ajouter la paire
supplémentaire pour le cadre et procéder
également comme pour la bande C.
Fond: remplissage no. 2.

KLETTE

Klöppel: 5 Paaze plus 1 paar
Konturfaden: 1 Paar

Mit 5 paaren Band C für die Mitte klöppeln.
Zusätzliches Paar für den Rahmen benutzen
und wie Band C klöppeln.
Füllung: Grund Nr. 2.

VOLOGODSKII CREEPER

Bobbins: 6 pairs
Gimps: 1 pair

Work tape A.
For the background guide see Fig.1.

Fig. 1

KLIMPLANT UIT VOLOGDA

Klossen: 6 paar
Sierdraden: 1 paar

Werk bandje A.
Voor de achtergrond: Fig. 1.

LIANE DE VOLOGDA

Fuseaux: 6 paires
Cordons: 1 paire

Faire la bande A.
Le dessin 1 indique comment faire le fond.

LIANE VON VOLOGDA

Klöppel: 6 Paare
Konturfäden: 1 Paar

Band A klöppeln.
Den Grund nach Abbildung 1 arbeiten.

BUTTERFLY BLUE IN FRAME

Bobbins: 5 pairs
Gimps: 1 pair

Work tape A.

There is no photograph of the
entire pattern as a finished piece
of lace, but the centre is shown
in the pattern on page 36.

BLAUWE VLINDER IN LIJST

Klossen: 5 paar
Sierdraden: 1 paar

Klos bandje A.
Er is geen foto van de totale kant, maar
het middenstuk is afgebeeld in het patroon
op blz. 36.

PAPILLON ENCADRE

Fuseaux: 5 paires
Cordons: 1 paire

Faire la bande A.
Il n'existe pas de photo de la dentelle
entière terminée, mais le centre est
visible au modèle à la page 36.

SCHMETTERLINGSKOMPOSTION
MIT RAHMEN

Klöppel: 5 Paare
Konturfäden: 1 Paar

Band A klöppeln.
Es gibt kein Foto der gesamten Arbeit als
fertige Spitze, jedoch die Mitte ist mit dem
Modell auf seite 36 gezeigt.

BABY BUTTERFLY IN FRAME

Bobbins: 5 pairs
Gimps: 1 pair

Work tape A.

Background: Filling note no. 2.
There is no photograph of the entire pattern as a finished
piece of lace, but the centre is shown in the pattern on
page 38.

KLEINE VLINDER IN LIJST

Klossen: 5 paar
Sierdraden: 1 paar

Klos bandje A.
Achtergrond: vullingaanwijzing
nr. 2.
Er is geen foto van de totale kant,
maar het middenstuk is afgebeeld
in het patroon op blz. 38.

BEBE PAPILLON ENCADRE

Fuseaux: 5 paires
Cordons: 1 paire

Faire la bande A.
Fond: remplissage no. 2.

Il n'existe pas de photo de la
dentelle entière terminée, mais le
centre est visible à la page 38.

SCHMETTERLINGSBABY
MIT RAHMEN

Klöppel: 5 Paare
Konturfäden: 1 Paar

Band A klöppeln.
Füllung: Grund Nr. 2.
Es gibt kein Foto der gesamten
Arbeit als fertige Spitze, jedoch
die Mitte ist mit dem Modell
auf seite 38 gezeigt.

ROCKING HORSE

Bobbins: 5 pairs
Gimps: 1 pair

Work tape B.
Background: Filling note no. 2.
There is no photograph of the entire
pattern as a finished piece of lace, but
the centre is shown in the pattern
on page 27.

HOBBELPAARD

Klossen: 5 paar
Sierdraden: 1 paar

Werk als bandje B.
Achtergrond: vullingaanwijzing nr. 2
Er ist geen foto van het geheel, maar het
middenstuk is afgebeeld in het patroon
op blz. 27.

CHEVAL A BASCULE

Fuseaux: 5 paires
Cordons: 1 paire

Faire la bande B.
Fond: remplissage no. 2
Il n'existe pas de photo de la dentelle
entière terminée, mais le centre est
visible au modèle à la page 27.

SCHAUKELPFERD

Klöppel: 5 Paare
Konturfäden: 1 Paar

Band B klöppeln.
Füllung: Grund Nr. 2.
Es gibt kein Foto der gesamten Arbeit
als fertige Spitze, jedoch die Mitte ist
mit dem Modell auf seite 27 gezeigt.

DANCING COCKEREL PANEL

Bobbins: 5 pairs
Gimps: 1 pair

Work tape A.
Background: Filling note no. 2.
There is no photograph of the entire pattern as
a finished piece of lace, but the centre is shown
in the pattern on page 26.

WANDKLEED MET DANSENDE HAAN

Klossen: 5 paar
Sierdraden: 1 paar

Klos bandje A.
Achtergrond: vullingaanwijzing nr. 2.
Er ist geen foto van het geheel, maar het
middenstuk is afgebeeld in het patroon
op blz. 26.

PANNEAU COQ QUI DANSE

Fuseaux: 5 paires
Cordons: 1 paire

Faire la bande A.
Fond: remplissage no. 2.
Il n'existe pas de photo de la dentelle
entière terminée, mais le centre est
visible au modèle à la page 26.

WANDBILD TÄNZELNDER HAHN

Klöppel: 5 Paare
Konturfäden: 1 Paar

Band A klöppeln.
Füllung: Grund Nr. 2.
Es gibt kein Foto der gesamten Arbeit
als fertige Spitze, jedoch die Mitte ist
mit dem Modell auf seite 26 gezeigt.

ANNA ANTONOVNA KORABLEVA

Born in 1918, Anna Korableva graduated at the Kalinin College of Art and Industry in Moscow in 1939. Following graduation, she became Director of the Scientific Research Institute of Art and Industry, where she worked as the leading artist for forty-five years.

Anna Korableva has created over one thousand individual art pieces of lace. These include measured laces, collars, handkerchiefs, tablecloths, and curtains. Amongst them she has produced a number of outstanding designs:

'The Little Birch Tree'
Birds
Ornament
Tile design
Russian motifs
Tablecloth designs
Matryoshkas
'The Rocking Horse'
'Satellite in Outer Space' (panel design)
'Cosmonauts' (souvenir design).

At a 1958 international exhibition in Brussels, she received the highest award – Grand Prix – for her curtain design 'Russian Motifs'. In 1970, at the Expo-70 in Japan, her curtain design 'Ornament' was displayed in the design exhibition, and in 1972, at an exhibition in the USA, her design 'The Flower' was displayed, for which she received a diploma.

Her creative works are on frequent display both in Russia and abroad, and she is a Serving Artist of Russia.

ANNA ANTONOVNA KORABLEVA

Anna Korableva is geboren in 1918. Ze studeerde in 1939 aan de Kalinin Academie voor Kunst en Industrie, in Moskou. Hierna werd ze directeur van het Instituut voor Wetenschappelijk Onderzoek voor Kunst en Industrie, waar ze vijf en veertig jaar werkte als artistiek leider.

Anna Korableva heeft meer dan duizend individuele kantkunstwerken gemaakt. Hieronder meterkanten, kragen, pochettes, tafelkleden en gordijnen. Hierbij heeft ze een aantal opvallende ontwerpen gemaakt:

"De kleine Beukeboom"
Vogels
Ornament
Tegelontwerp
Russische motieven
Ontwerpen voor tafelkleden
Matryoshkas
"Het Hobbelpaard"
"Satelliet in de Ruimte" (ontwerp voor een wandkleed)
"Kosmonauten" (ontwerp voor souvenirs).

Bij een internationale tentoonstelling in Brussel in 1958, kreeg ze de hoogste prijs – Grand Prix – voor haar gordijnontwerp "Russische Motieven". Tijdens de Expo-70 in Japan, in 1970, werd haar gordijnontwerp "Ornament" tentoongesteld in de ontwerpentoonstelling, en in 1972, was haar ontwerp "De Bloem" te zien op een tentoonstelling in de Verenigde Staten, waarvoor ze een oorkonde kreeg.

Haar creatieve werk wordt regelmatig tentoongesteld zowel binnen Rusland als daarbuiten, en ze is "Serving Artist of Russia" (Kunstenaar van Verdienste in Rusland).

ANNA ANTONOVNA KORABLEVA

Née en 1918, Anna Korableva a obtenu sa licence au Collège Kalinin des Arts et de l'Industrie, à Moscou, en 1939. Après cet examen, elle a été promue Directrice de l'Institut Scientifique des Arts et de l'Industrie, où elle a tenu un rôle prépondérant comme artiste pendant quarante-cinq ans.

Anna Korableva a créé plus d'un millier de pièces d'art individuelles en dentelle, comprenant de la dentelle au mètre, des cols, des pochettes, des nappes et des rideaux. Parmi eux, elle a produit un nombre important de dessins remarquables:

"Le petit bouleau"
Oiseaux
Ornement
Dessin de tuiles
Motifs russes
Desins de nappes
Matrioschkas
"Le cheval à bascule"
"Satelitte dans l'espace" (dessin pour panneau)
"Cosmonautes" (dessin commémoratif).

A l'Exposition Internationale de Bruxelles en 1958, la plus haute récompense – le Grand Prix – lui a été décerné pour son dessin de rideau "Motifs russes". En 1970, à l'Expo-70 au Japon, son rideau "Ornement" a été montré dans la section des dessins et, en 1972, elle a reçu un diplôme pour son dessin "La Fleur" lors d'une exposition aux USA.

Ses travaux créatifs continuent à être exposés aussi bien en Russie que dans d'autres pays, et elle est toujours une artiste active de la Russie.

ANNA ANTONOVNA KORABLEVA

Im Jahre 1918 geboren, machte Anna Korableva 1939 an der Kalinin-Hochschule für Kunst und Industrie in Moskau ihr Examen. Danach wurde sie Leiterin des Foschungsinstitutes für Kunst und Industrie, wo sie als führende Künstlerin 45 Jahre lang wirkte.

Anna Korableva schuf über eintausend einzigartiger Kunstwerke in Spitze. Diese umfassen Meterspitzen, Krägen, Taschentücher, Tischtücher und Vorhänge. Unter ihnen entwarf sie einige hervorragende Muster:

"Die kleine Birke"
Vögel
Ornament
Ziegelmuster
russische Motive
Matrioschkas
"Das Schaukelpferd"
"Satellit im Weltraum" (Wandbild)
"Kosmonauten" (Gedenk-Schöpfung).

Bei der internationalen Auustellung in Brüssel erhielt sie 1958 die höchste Auszeichnung – den Grand Prix – für ihren Vorhangentwurf "Russische Motive". Im Jahre 1970 wurde ihr Entwurf "Ornament" anlässlich der Zeichnung-Ausstellung von Expo-70 in Japan gezeigt, und bei einer Ausstellung in den USA erhielt ihr Werk "Die Blume" eine Auszeichnung.

Ihre schöpferischen Arbeiten werden sowohl in Russland wie auch in anderen Ländern weiterhin ausgestellt, und als aktive Künstlerin steht sie immer noch im Dienste Russlands.

SOURCES OF INFORMATION

United Kingdom

The Lace Guild
The Hollies
53 Audnam
Stourbridge
West Midlands DY8 4AE

OIDFA
Jean Barrett
71 The Oval
Brookfield
Middlesborough
Cleveland TS5 8EZ

The British College
of Lace
21 Hillmorton Road
Rugby
Warwickshire CV22 5DF

International Old Lacers
Ann Keller
Cool Valley
Abingdon Park
Shankill
Dublin

The Lacemakers' Circle
49 Wardwick
Derby DE1 1HY

The Lace Society
Lynwood
Stratford Road
Oversley, Alcester
Warwickshire B49 6PG

Ring of Tatters
Miss B. Netherwood
269 Oregon Way
Chaddesden
Derby DE21 6UR

Australia

Australian Lace Guild
National Committee
Box Hill
Victoria 3128

Australian Lace Magazine
P.O. Box 609
Manly
NSW 2095

Belgium

OIDFA
Lydia Thiels-Mertens
Jagersberg 1
B-3294 Molenstede-Diest

Belgische Kantorganisatie
Irma Boone
Gentse Steenweg 296
B-9240 Zele

France

OIDFA
Suzanne Puech
3 Chemin de Parenty
F-69250 Neuville sur
Saône

Germany

OIDFA
Uta Ulrich
Papenbergweg 33
D-32756 Detmold

Deutscher
Klöppelverband e.V
Schulstr. 38
D-52531 Übach
Palenberg

Klöppelschule
Nordhalben
Klöppelschule 4
D-96365 Nordhalben

The Netherlands

OIDFA
Elly De Vries
Couwenhoven 52-07
NL-3703 ER Zeist

LOKK
Boterbloem 56
NL-7322 GX Apeldoorn

Switzerland

Fédération de
Dentellières
Suisses
Evelyne Lütolf
Buhnstrasse 12
CH-8052 Zürich

USA

OIDFA
Elaine Merritt
5915 Kyburz Place
San José CA 95120
Illinois 60091

International Old Lacers
Box 557
Flanders
NJ 07836

Point Ground Tours &
Publications
124 W. Irvington Place
Denver
Co 80223-1539

OIDFA

(International Bobbin
and Needle
Lace Organization)

President
Lydia Thiels-Mertens
Jagersberg 1
B-3294 Molenstede-Diest
Belgium

Vice President
Alice De Smedt
Welvaartstraat 149
B-Aalst
Belgium

SUPPLIERS

England

BEDFORDSHIRE

Arthur Sells
49 Pedley Lane
Clifton
Shefford SG17 5QT

BERKSHIRE

Chrisken
26 Cedar Drive
Kingsclere RG20 5TD

BUCKINGHAMSHIRE

Bartlett Caesar Partners
The Lace Studio
12 Creslow Court
Galley Hill
Stoney Stratford
Milton Keynes
MK11 1NN

J.S. Sear
Lacecraft Supplies
8 Hillview
Sherington MK16 9NJ

Winslow Bobbins
70 Magpie Way
Winslow MK18 3PZ

SMP Lace
The Lace Workshop
1 Blays, Churchfield Road
Chalfont St Peter SL9 0HB

CAMBRIDGESHIRE

Josie and Jeff Harrison
(*Lace Pillows*)
Walnut Cottage
Winwick
Huntingdon PE17 5PN

Heffers Graphic Shop
(*matt coloured transparent
adhesive film*)
19 Sidney Street
Cambridge CB2 3HL

Spangles, the Bead People
Carole Morris
1 Casburn Lane
Burwell CB5 0ED

CHESHIRE

Lynn Turner (*mail order,
and general supplies*)
Church Meadow Crafts
3 Woodford Lane
over Winsford
CW7 2JS

DEVON

Honiton Lace Shop
44 High Street
Honiton EX14 8PJ

DORSET

Frank Herring & Sons
27 High West Street
Dorchester DT1 1UP

T. Parker (*mail order,
general supplies and bobbins*)
124 Corhampton Road
Boscombe East
Bournemouth BH6 5NZ

ESSEX

Mainly Lace
Moulsham Mill
Parkway
Chelmsford
Essex CM2 7PX

GLOUCESTERSHIRE

Evelyn and Tony Brown
(*Pillow makers*)
Temple Lane Cottage
Littledean
GL14 3NX

Chosen Crafts Centre
46 Winchcombe Street
Cheltenham GL52 2ND

HERTFORDSHIRE

Barleycroft Lacemaking
Supplies, 'Honeypuddle'
13 Barleycroft
Stevenage SG2 9NP

HUMBERSIDE

Sandra's Handpainted Bobbins
Sandra Fields
31 Seacroft Road
Cleethorpes DN35 0AX

ISLE OF WIGHT

Busy Bobbins
Unit 7
Scarrots Lane
Newport PO30 1JD

KENT

D.J. Hornsby
25 Manwood Avenue
Canterbury CT2 7AH

Francis Iles
73 High Street
Rochester ME1 1LX

MERSEYSIDE

Hayes & Finch
Head Office and Factory
Hanson Road
Aintree
Liverpool L9 9BP

MIDDLESEX

Redburn Crafts
Squires Garden Centre
Halliford Road
Upper Halliford
Shepperton TW17 8RU

NORFOLK

Stitches and Lace
Alby Craft Centre
Cromer Road
Alby
Norwich NR11 7QE

Breklaw Crafts
The Corner Shop
Rickinghall, Diss
IP22 1EG

NORTHAMPTONSHIRE

Anna's Lace Chest
1 Gorse Close
Whitehills
Northants NN2 8ED

Teazle Embroideries
35 Boothferry Road
Hull

Teazle Embroideries
35 Boothferry Road
Hull

STAFFORDSHIRE

John & Jennifer Ford
(*mail order, and lace days only*)
October Hill
Upper Longdon
Rugeley WS15 1QB

SUFFOLK

A.R. Archer (*bobbins*)
Yew Tree Cottage
High Street
Walsham Le Willows
Bury St Edmunds

Mary Collings (*linen by
the metre, and made-up
articles of church linen*)
Church Furnishings
St Andrews Hall
Humber Doucy Lane
Ipswich IP4 3BP

Stephen Pearce
Yew Tree Cottage
Chapel Road
Grundisburgh
Woodbridge IP13 6TS

Piper Silks
(*specialist silk yarns*)
'Chinnery's'
Egremont Street
Glemsford
CO10 7SA

SURREY

Needle and Thread
80 High Street
Horsell
Woking GU21 4SZ

SUSSEX

Southern Handicrafts
20 Kensington Gardens
Brighton BN1 4AC

WARWICKSHIRE

Christine & David
Springett
21 Hillmorton Road
Rugby CV22 5DF

WEST MIDLANDS

Acorn Bobbins
Eric Sutton
2 Roman Road
Stoke
Coventry CV2 4LD

Framecraft Miniatures Ltd
372-376 Summer Lane
Hockley
Birmingham B19 3QA

The Needlewoman
21 Needless Alley
off New Street
Birmingham B2 5AE

Stitches
Dovehouse Shopping
Parade
335 Warwick Road
Olton, Solihull

YORKSHIRE

The Craft House
22 Bar Street
Scarborough YO11 2HT

Jo Firth
Lace Making &
Needlecraft Supplies
58 Kent Crescent
Lowtown
Pudsey LS28 9EB

Just Lace
Lacemaker Supplies
14 Ashwood Gardens
Gildersome
Leeds LS27 7AS

Sebalace
Waterloo Mill
Howden Road
Silsden BD20 0HA

D.H. Shaw
47 Lamor Crescent
Thrushcroft
Rotherham S66 9QD

Stitchery
6 Finkle Street
Richmond
DL10 4QA

George White
Lacemaking Supplies
40 Heath Drive
Boston Spa LS23 6PB

WILTSHIRE

Doreen Campbell
(*frames and mounts*)
Highcliff
Bremilham Road
Malmesbury SN16 0DQ

Scotland

Christine Riley
53 Barclay Street
Stonehaven
Kincardineshire

Peter & Beverley Scarlett
Strupak
Hill Head
Cold Wells, Ellon
Grampion

Wales

Bryncraft Bobbins
B.J. Phillips
Pantglas
Cellan
Lampeter
Dyfed SA48 8JD

Hilkar Lace Suppliers
(*mail order, and
lace days only*)
33 Mysydd Road
Landore
Swansea SA1 2NZ

Australia

Dentelles Lace Supplies
c/o Betty Franks
36 Lang Terrace
Northgate 4013
Brisbane
Queensland

Kipparra Lace Supplies
'Clear Oaks'
Margaret Livingstone
135 Francis Street
Richmond NSW 2753

Lace Craft
Valerie Dunsmore
3 Barton Drive
Mount Eliza
Victoria 3930

Lace Inspirations
Joanne Pope
16 Robertson Road
Leopold
Victoria 3224

J.O. O'Brien
61 Bligh Avenue
Camden
NSW 2570

Annette and John Pollard
1 Panorama Road
Penrith
NSW 2750

Randwick Art and Craft
Supplies
203 Avoca Street
Randwick
NSW 2031

Belgium

't Handwerkhuisje
Katelijnestraat 23
8000 Bruges

Kantcentrum
Peperstraat 3A
8000 Bruges

Manufacture Belge de
Dentelle
6 Galerie de la Reine
Galeries Royales St Hubert
1000 Bruxelles

Orchidée
Mariastraat 18
8000 Bruges

Orchidée N.V.
Fabricage + Groothandel
Blankenbergsesteenweg
65a
8377 Zuienkerke-Brugge

Ann Thys
't Apostelientje
Balstraat 11
8000 Bruges

'Scharlaeken'
J. Vandenweghe
Philipstockstraat 5
B-8000

France

La Galerie
Centre d'Enseignement à
la Dentelle Au Fuseau
1 Rue Raphaël
43000 Le Puy en Velay

A L'Econome
Anne-Marie Deydier
Ecole de Dentelle aux
Fuseaux
10 rue Paul Chenavard
69001 Lyon

Rougier et Plé
13-15 bd des Filles de
Calvaire
75003 Paris

Germany

Barbara Fay Verlag &
Versandbuchhandlung
Am Goosberg 2
D-24340 Gammelby

Rittersgrüner
Klöppelboutique
Barbara Neubert
Karlsbader Str. 43
D-08355 Rittersgrün

Werkstatt Textil
Ellen Meyer
An der Obertrave 42
D-23552 Lübeck

The Netherlands

Theo Brejaart
Dordtselaan 146
P.O. Box 5199
3008 AD Rotterdam

Heikina de Rüyter
Zuiderstraat 1
9693 ER Nieuweschans

Magazijn De Vlijt
Lijnmarkt 48
3511 KJ Utrecht

Tiny van Donschot
Dries 95
6006 Al Weert

New Zealand

Peter McLeavey
P.O. Box 69.007
Auckland 8

Switzerland

Buchhandlung
Scheidegger & Co. AG
Obere Bahnhofstr. 10A
CH-8910 Affoltern a.A.

Martin Burkhard
Klöppelzubehör
Jurastrasse 7
CH-5300 Turgi

Fädehax
Irene Solcà
Lolcherstrasse 7
CH-7000 Chur

USA

Arbor House
22 Arbor Lane
Roslyn Heights
NY 11577

Baltazor Fabrics and Lace
3262 Severn Avenue
Metairie
LA 7002-4848

Beggars' Lace
P.O. Box 481223
Denver
CO 80248

Berga Ullman Inc.
P.O. Box 918
North Adams
MA 01247

Forget Me Knot
17828 Bellflower Blvd
Bellflower
CA 90706

Handy Hands
Rt. 1, Box 4
Paxton
Il 6095

Happy Hands
3007 S.W. Marshall
Pendleton
OR 97180

J & R Hensell
P.O. Box 825
Marcola
OR 97454-0825

International Old Lacers
Inc.
124 West Irvington Place
Denver
CO 80223-1539

The Lacemaker
176 Sunset Ave S.
P.O. Box 77525
Edmonds
WA 98177-525

Lacis
3163 Adeline Street
Berkeley
CA 94703

Laurik's Lacemaking
Supplies
3790 El Camino Real Suite
103
Palo Alto
CA 94306

Robin's Bobbins
Murphy Highway
Mineral Bluff
GA 30559-9736

Robin and Russ
Handweavers
533 North Adams Street
McMinnville
OR 97128

Snowgoose
1880
S. Pierce 4
Lakewood
CO 80232

Unicorn Books
Glimakra Looms 'n
Yarns Inc.
1304 Scott Street
Petaluma
CA 94954-1181

Unique Apparel
6501 E 113th Street
Kansas City
MO 64134

The Unique and
Art Lace Cleaners
5926 Delman Boulevard
St Louis
MO 63112

Van Sciver Bobbin Lace
130 Cascadilla Park
Ithaca
NY 14850

The World in Stitches
82 South Street
Milford
NR 03055

INDEX